The Benidorm Guide

to a Happy Holiday

Derren Litten

CONSTABLE

Constable & Robinson Ltd., 55–56 Russell Square, London WC1B 4HP. www.constablerobinson.com
First published in the UK by Constable, an imprint of Constable & Robinson Ltd., 2011.
Copyright © Derren Litten / Tiger Aspect Productions Limited, 2011.   Book designed by unreal-uk.com
The right of Derren Litten to be identified as the author of this work has been asserted by him in accordance with the Copyright,
Designs & Patents Act 1988.

A copy of the British Library Cataloguing in Publication Data is available from the British Library
UK ISBN: 978-1-78033-243-7   Printed and bound in Italy
Photographs courtesy of Rex Features: page 3 (both), 4 (both), 5 (top), 16 (all), 17 (all), 30 (bottom, left and right), 40 (all), 41 (all).
All other images courtesy of Tiger Aspect Productions, Unreal Ltd or Shutterstock.

for Geoffrey Perkins

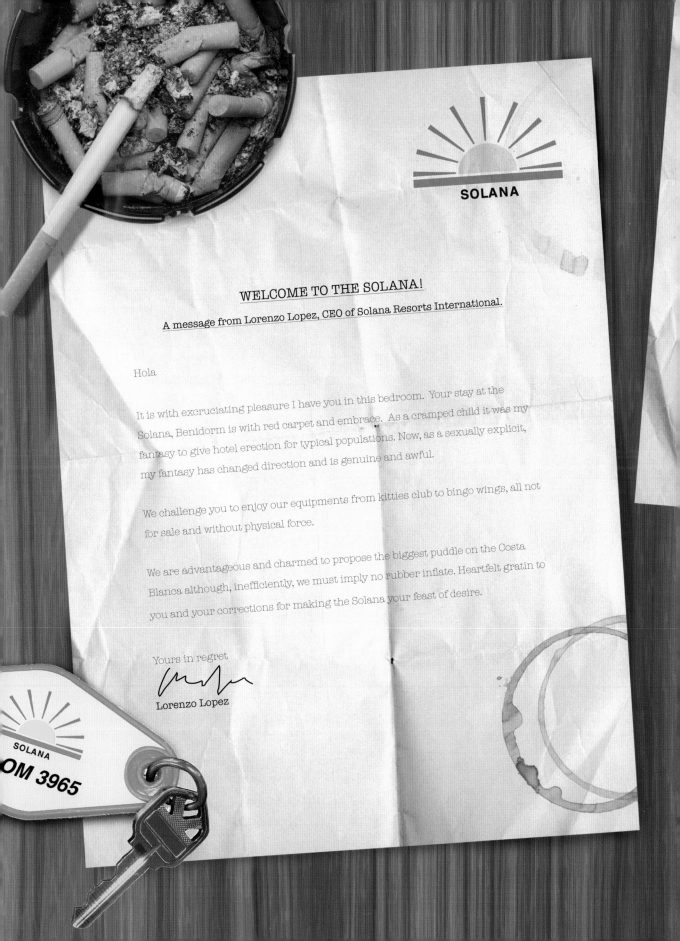

WELCOME TO THE SOLANA!

A message from Lorenzo Lopez, CEO of Solana Resorts International.

Hola

It is with excruciating pleasure I have you in this bedroom. Your stay at the Solana, Benidorm is with red carpet and embrace. As a cramped child it was my fantasy to give hotel erection for typical populations. Now, as a sexually explicit, my fantasy has changed direction and is genuine and awful.

We challenge you to enjoy our equipments from kitties club to bingo wings, all not for sale and without physical force.

We are advantageous and charmed to propose the biggest puddle on the Costa Blanca although, inefficiently, we must imply no rubber inflate. Heartfelt gratin to you and your corrections for making the Solana your feast of desire.

Yours in regret

Lorenzo Lopez

'The
the fu

HELLO, MADGE HARVEY (nee Barron) here to talk about the controversial subject of tanning. First of all let's get one thing out of the way, this subject is **NOT controversial, the sun is GOOD for you, not bad.**

In the last few years a load of pale, often vegetarian, moaning minnies have tried to persuade the general public that getting a good sun tan is actually bad for your health. Hahahaha, these people do make me laugh, it's the same lot that say smoking is bad for you too. As my husband Mel used to say, *"It's political correctness gone mad."* First of all let us look at some people in the public eye who have a nice, healthy tan and then at some others who are pale; let's see which look weak and miserable and which look successful and glamorous.

future's bright, ture's orange'

LOOK AT HIS TEETH!

This is George Hamilton IV. Some of the younger readers might not recognise him but he was a GLAMOROUS and RICH film star. He looked a bit like Warren Beatty but with a darker sun tan, so obviously, more attractive. Look at his teeth. Not many people know this but George Hamilton IV has very bad teeth but next to that wonderful sun kissed skin they look pearly white. Why do you think black people always look like they've got nice teeth? (And before you say anything, that wasn't racist, that was a nice thing to say.)

Des O'Connor has always been one of my favourites: he's a wonderful singer and can also tell a good joke (sometimes risque but never blue). Just look at his healthy, smiling face. He's smiling because he's happy, he's happy because he's got a nice healthy tan. (Also worth knowing: his songs are great for karaoke as you don't really have to be able to sing, my husband Mel did a great Dik-a-Dum-Dum).

DIK-A-DUM-DUM!

MADGE'S TOP TANNING TIPS

LITTLE LAD CALLED KENNY

Now I thought they were taking the piss when they gave me this picture, but apparently this little lad is called Kenny Osbourne and he actually leaves the house like this on days other than Halloween. Honestly, the kids these days. Apparently he's not actually a celebrity himself but his father is famous as he used to be a werewolf and his mother was a judge on *New Faces*. If you are pale GET YOURSELF OUT IN THE SUN, no amount of make up (clown or otherwise) is going to distract from the fact that you look like you are dying. If you can't afford a holiday in Spain get yourself to a sun bed shop, there really is no excuse.

Now I don't know who this lovely lad and lass are but you can tell from their healthy tans that they are HAPPY and SUCCESSFUL. OK, he looks a bit of a porker but I don't think he looks English so eating a lot is probably part of his culture. It's a proven fact that pale people are unattractive and usually poor. This couple don't look short of a bob or two and with their healthy tans and their bulging wallets are obviously destined to live happily ever after.

BIT OF A PORKER!

SOMETIMES
A PICTURE
IS WORTH A
THOUSAND
WORDS. NOW,
DO YOU STILL
WANT TO SIT IN
THE SHADE?

TOO MUCH SUN?

The answer to this question is simple, you can never have too much sun. It's a proven fact that if you do get burnt you just need a couple of days to recover. However if you are on a weekend break somewhere sunny and get burnt on the first day DO NOT stay out of the sun the next day, get yourself out there and lap up them rays. If you are going home to a rainy, wet, grey, miserable summer GET ANOTHER DAY'S SUN WHILE YOU CAN. Yes, it'll sting a bit but at least you won't be going home pale and depressed. Look at this lovely lass who went on a weekend trip to Fuengirola, that rawness will go down in a few days and just think how embarrassed she would have been to go back to work all pale after bragging for weeks on end that she was gonna have a couple of days in the sun.

MADGE'S TOP TANNING TOOLS

1. Face reflector Essential to get that crispy brown look to your sun kissed face. **2. Timer** A good idea if you have only one day of sun, make sure you get a good tan front and back. **3. Sun cream** I tend not to bother with a sun cream to be honest but I've lately found that a good quality cooking oil can give you a lovely sizzle. **4. Cigarettes** 5 or 6 hours in the sun can be quite a marathon so I find a nice cigarette every few minutes tends to cool me down.

"A HEALTHY 9.5, LIKE ANOTHER CERTAIN PART OF MY ANATOMY"

Mick

Full name:
Mick Garvey.

Place & date of birth:
Lancashire, UK. 01.04.68.

Occupation:
Bit of this, bit of that.

Favourite holiday destination & why?
Benidorm, it's like Blackpool with sun.

Favourite food?
I'm a meat and 2 veg man (although I wouldn't go around saying that in the old town of Benidorm).

Karaoke song?
"Ain't No Pleasing You" by Chas & Dave.

Which TV shows do you watch?
Anything except bloody soaps, my wife is glued to them.

Do you have a role model?
Brad Pitt, we have so much in common.

If you had to rate yourself 1–10 in attractiveness, how would you score?
A healthy 9.5, like another certain part of my anatomy.

What has been your greatest accomplishment in life?
This questionnaire, nearly bored the arse off me.

WHACKY RACES
Mobility Scooters to Hire or Buy

Whacky Races, Benidorm's premier mobility scooter rental outlet is proud to have been serving the disabled, infirm and just plain lazy holiday maker since 1994.

It's charge and go with our (almost) fully insured fleet of top notch scooters, electric wheelchairs and them funny walking frames on wheels that look like something out of *Star Wars*. Our dedicated and partly trained staff are here to advise you on what make and model is right for you.

Wide Eyed And Legless – €60 per week
This is our premier range of scooters, for people who aren't just lazy, their legs don't actually work. These beauties can practically climb stairs (because you can't).

Baby Just Cares For Me – €40 per week
This is our slightly less flexible range for people who can actually walk but feel they don't want to; and why not, you've saved all year for this holiday, you're entitled to a rest. Some of these models are slightly older and may require a push start.

Stormy Weather – €80 per week
Fully protected by the elements, this totally enclosed mobility scooter is ideal for those unpredictable Benidorm thunderstorms. Chain smokers please be aware, there is no ventilation in this vehicle, none at all.

Little Ol' Wine Drinker Me – €25 per week
Ideal for the wizened alcoholic, this lightweight framed scooter (carries up to 7 stone in weight) can reach speeds of up to 20mph. Perfect for when you need to rush out to the off licence for that cheap bottle of brandy before they close for one of those annoying siestas. Front wire basket can hold up to eight cans of super strength lager.

Three Times A Lady – €100 per week
Whether it's glandular or gluttony we don't judge, you'd need an arse as big as a paddling pool to not fit into one of our SuperSize range of mobility scooters. Each mega scooter can hold a person up to 25 stone in weight (although no heavier than this, we don't cater for freaks). Optional thermos heated trailer, can house up to 16 meat pies/pasties or two generous takeaway orders.

We're only a phone call away, free delivery in the Benidorm area.

Tel: +34 054542 45424 – Open 7 days a week, 9am – 7pm
22 Avenida de Bazooka, Benidorm, Alicante, Spain
(Opposite Clucky Fried Chicken)

DONALD & JACQUELINE'S

Holiday Wordsearch

HOLIDAY	FLIGHT	FOOD	POOL
GREECE	BENIDORM	RELAX	BUCKET
SAND	HOT	VALUE	SPADE
BEACH	SHADE	SPAIN	CHEAP
RENTAL	SUN	BED	DEAL

E	S	I	N	E	P	T	V	M	M	V	A	G	S	A
L	P	B	F	E	L	C	H	R	U	D	P	A	P	K
A	U	T	L	K	C	O	C	O	C	K	S	Y	A	N
T	N	D	I	L	D	O	H	D	S	P	H	D	E	O
N	K	C	G	T	X	B	E	I	D	O	O	F	T	C
E	S	L	H	C	W	V	A	N	A	O	L	I	C	K
R	M	O	T	A	S	A	P	E	C	L	I	G	S	E
B	T	C	N	U	R	L	N	B	K	S	D	A	U	R
F	U	K	N	S	P	U	N	K	H	C	A	E	B	S
M	E	M	E	N	B	E	R	T	G	L	Y	A	E	H
R	A	I	M	U	F	F	I	N	N	R	A	T	D	A
T	H	R	E	E	S	O	M	E	E	I	E	E	O	D
D	G	M	D	O	R	I	O	L	I	K	A	E	D	E
N	F	A	N	N	Y	T	A	R	C	A	C	P	C	S
A	P	S	Y	N	O	X	I	U	G	E	P	H	S	E
S	E	X	T	I	T	S	B	T	X	Y	K	S	E	X

Is it free?
¿Está libre?

Do you do discount?
¿Usted hace descuento?

A pound to have a shit on the plane?!
¡Una libra para tener una mierda en un avión?!

Why do I bother?
¿Por qué intento?

Let's get pisspero'ed on Nisspero.
Consigamos pisspero'ed en Nisspero.

It's like Blackpool with sun.
Es como Blackpool con el sol.

Can I borrow your mobile? I'm out of credit.
¿Puedo pedir prestado su móvil? Estoy fuera de crédito.

Are you taking the piss?
¿Usted está tomando el piss?

These are our sunbeds.
Éstos son nuestros sunbeds.

What time does the karaoke start?
¿Hacen cuándo hicieron el comienzo del Karaoke?

Mick

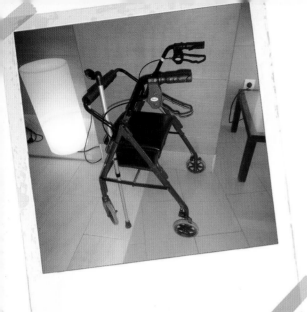

SHITE
SNAPS

Noreen's Holi

Hola!

NOREEN MALTBY HERE, WISHING YOU A LOVELY HAPPY HOLIDAY, WHEREVER IN THE WORLD YOU HAPPEN TO BE GOING. ONE THING'S FOR SURE, WHILE TRAVELLING TO YOUR DESTINATION OF CHOICE THE ODD IMPROMPTU GAME CERTAINLY HELPS TO PASS THE TIME. HERE ARE A FEW OF MY FAVOURITES.

A rare win for Team Noreen

I Spy Oh this is a classic! Possibly my all time favourite game, but you needn't limit yourself to spying an object that you can actually see around you at the time (S for swimming pool, B for BBQ, F for flip flops, etc). Apparently, if you know the history of the area where you are you can include objects that "would" have been there in days gone by. Our Geoff came up with this rule when I'd been trying to guess something beginning with "Z" for about four days around the Solana swimming pool. Turns out it was "zombie". Being a stickler for the rules I pulled Geoff up on this as there was no zombie around the pool at the time of playing the game (although to be fair Madge had fallen asleep in the shade and didn't look too clever). But Geoff then told me the Solana pool was built on the site of an eighteenth-century Spanish graveyard and there was probably more zombies underneath it than there was lilos on top of it! Amazing what you can learn when you spend a bit of time with our Geoff.

Eddie Stobart This is a great little game and again, just so easy to play. On a long car journey if you see an Eddie

Geoff and me

Stobart truck pass by your window you have to shout out, "Eddie Stobart!" If you shout it out first you win the point*. That's all there is to it! Oh we do have a laugh! (Not so great on plane journeys this one).*I've never quite fully fathomed out the point system on this one as on the few occasions I've ended up with more points than Geoff he often plays "Crabbit's rule" which means the points are "inversed on the diagonal" and I end up losing. Oh he's a clever boy, I'm that proud of him …

I scream Ice Scream!

What a laugh this is. If you happen to find yourself outside the vicinity of your all inclusive, at any time you feel like an ice cream all you have to do is shout "ICE CREAM, ICE CREAM, ICE CREAM", three times like that at the top of your voice then the other person has to pay! Apparently you have to pick your moments though as I found out on a day trip to London when I screamed "ICE CREAM, ICE CREAM, ICE CREAM" at the top of my voice about 10 minutes before the interval of *War Horse*. Ooh, there's some miserable types in that London I tell you.

Oh we do have a laugh!

Underwater Challenge Our Geoff got the idea for this one after reading a magazine article about Houdini and that magician who seems a bit slow, I can't remember his name, David somebody. Anyway, apparently Houdini and Slow David both did a trick where they held their breath under water for, oh, about three minutes I think it was, something death defying like that. Anyway, every time we go on holiday now Geoff jumps in the pool and has a crack at beating the record. Great fun but make sure you remember to set the timer properly. I'm a devil for messing it up and my goodness when Geoff surfaces gasping for air after nearly killing himself and he finds out I forgot to start the stop watch or I fell asleep, boy can he turn the air blue! A bit like his face after him doing the challenge!

Psychic Scrabble Although not impromptu, this is a version of Scrabble our Geoff told me about which proves an interesting variation on the original. It all started when, by some miracle, I beat Geoff at Scrabble two games in a row; oh he was upset but then he calmed down when he remembered 'Psychic Scrabble', apparently invented by the psychic and professional bender Uni Geller. Basically it follows the rules of proper Scrabble except if you play a word and the opposing player knew you were going to play it because of a premonition he'd had a few seconds before then you forfeit your turn and miss a turn. I thought it was a bit strange that Geoff never just told me the word BEFORE I played it (you'd think if he was psychic he could) but apparently it doesn't work like that. I'm not surprised I couldn't work it out, I've never been very good with the occult; I thought my star sign was Sagittarius with asparagus rising.

Imaginary Dice This is one my son Geoff made up. It's such a lot of fun and so easy to do. Basically each person has an imaginary dice, each player throws his/her dice and announces to the other player(s) what his score was. The person with the lowest score has to stay silent for 10 minutes. Then you start again. If you both throw a six you just keep throwing until someone has a score that beats the other person. Our Geoff has absolutely incredible luck with this game, I hope you do too!

FILM 2011

with Mick Garvey

Everyone knows the best holidays to go on are all inclusive but what happens when the entertainment stops? Yes, the drinks are all inclusive but you can find yourself at a loose end when they call time at 1 a.m. Yes, of course you could go out on the town but that would cost MONEY and if you start all them shenanigans you can see the cost of your holidays soaring close to £1,000 for a family of five (as in the words of Peter Andre, this is insania).

So, here's what you do: borrow a laptop from a well off friend and have a good stock of quality movies to watch (nothing too taxing, we're talking more *Bucket List* than *Schindler's*).

And I know what you're going to say, what about the cost of the DVDs. DVDs? Don't make me laugh, download them off the internet like everybody else does!

Mick's Top holiday fil

10 **Groundhog Day** This film is about a guy who wakes up up every day and has basically the same day, the same things happen to him day in day out, exactly the same things. If it was set on holiday in a Benidorm all-inclusive there would be nothing remarkable about this film at all. We get up with a splitting headache, find the same sun beds, have a drink to settle the shakes, have our dinner, have an argument, swim in the pool, have our tea, get drunk, sing the same karaoke songs, go to bed. Somehow they make *Groundhog Day* a brilliant and very funny film; obviously if they did a movie about our time in Benidorm it was be boring, repetitive and not really funny at all.

9 **Avatar** This is bloody mental. It's about a planet populated by nine-foot, blue aliens. Even Madge my mother in law couldn't come up with this kind of shit and she's taken acid. There is a soppy love story (with a fair bit of alien action, if that's your thing) but don't worry, there's loads of killings and brilliant special effects as well. There is a moral to the story like all Hollywood films; basically it's "You can't stand in the way of progress". We had a similar thing when protesters were banging on about the council putting a bypass through a load of fields near us. At the end of the day hippies need to practise what they preach and CHILL OUT; you may be complaining now 'cause they're chopping down trees but let's see what you have to say when you've nothing to wipe your arse on.

10 films

3 **The Godfather Parts I, II & III** Absolute classics. Any film where someone wakes up with a horse's head in their bed has got to rate pretty highly. I once thought someone had put an animal's head in one of our beds on holiday but it just turned out to be Madge having a lie in. I once had a run in with the Mafia myself although it wasn't like this; it all happened in a weird Western film set, then went on to a race track where Madge was challenged to a go kart race for three thousand euros with … oh forget it, you wouldn't believe me anyway.

2 **Cool Hand Luke** I never used to bother with prison films, I mean how can you top *Porridge*? I don't mean with jam or nuts and raisins, I mean how can you top the TV series *Porridge* but apparently you can. Admittedly there are a few dodgy prison movies where they all just end up bumming each other (I think one of them had that Louis Theroux in it) but two of the best are *Escape From Altringham* and this one, *Cool Hand Luke*. I think my favourite scene is where some-body bets Paul Newman (Luke) that he can't eat 50 boiled eggs in under an hour. Of course he does it, absolute piece of piss; I've seen some people do that at an all-you-can-eat breakfast in Benidorm in far less time and nobody bet them to do it.

8 **Blazing Saddles** Brilliant cowboys and Indians film that goes a bit mad at the end. Of all the films I've seen where a man punches a horse in the face this is definitely in the top three. Most of the humour is what my wife would call "lavatorial" (farting, people shitting themselves, etc.) and there will, naturally, be those who don't find this kind of thing amusing (these people are known as "miseries", not to be confused with that fat bird who squashed James Caan's legs in the movie of the same name). Those of you who do have a sense of humour will agree with me when I say anyone who doesn't think farting is funny should be made to watch this film while our Michael sits on their knee after eating boiled egg curry with a side order of mushy peas.

7 **The Matrix** Well, your guess is as good as mine as to what this is all about but it's brilliant. Why have a fight sequence with two people when you can have the same fight with fifty of the same people! I mean it's the same person but they have doubles. Not stunt doubles, I mean the exact same person but there's more of them (I told you it was complicated). Don't worry about the storyline, there isn't one really, it's just about a geeky lad who is into computers, then it all goes a bit mental. Great to watch when you're tanked up but to be honest if you're watching these film on holiday you're hardly gonna be sober are you?

6 **High School Musical** Shit but it keeps the kids quiet.

5 **Brief Encounter** See the review above but replace the word "kids" with wife or mother in law.

4 **Perfume** I know, I know, you're sitting there thinking, "A film about perfume? Has Mick completely lost it?" But believe me there is method in my madness. This film has more tits than Bill Oddie's garden. And because of the name the missus will be up for watching it too. Just don't look too excited when the jugs come out.

1 **Carry On Abroad & Camping** These are the ultimate holiday films. Rubbished in their day for being, well, rubbish; they are now considered cult classics. I've never really understood what the word cult means I know a word very much like it (in fact my mother in law is more or less the definition of it) but don't really know what cult means. If it means nobody watched the movies that's not true, these films raked it in at the box office. If it means they are weird, they're not, they're just piss funny. I think it means posh people don't like them so instead of admitting they are good they have to lump them into a weird category with crap films and films that sold about 4 copies on DVD. Rainy day in Benidorm? You have two choices, either stick one of these films on the laptop or just look out of the window, you'll see pretty much the same thing!

Lesley's

TOP TEN HOLIDAY COCKTAILS

Witches Tit

Sambucca, grenadine,
cherry to garnish

Hot Vomit

Southern Comfort, gin,
soda water, 2 raw eggs,
tinned sweetcorn,
topped up with boiling water

Angry Dwarf

Vodka, Tabasco, angostura bitters,
Worcestershire sauce, Twiglet swizzle stick

Gay Derek

Pink gin, pomegranate liqueur,
pineapple, cocktail umbrella

Horny Monkey
Banana liqueur, Malibu,
shot of liquid Viagra

Flat Battery

Ginger beer, single malt whisky,
absinthe, raw ginger swizzle stick

Big Donna
Chocolate milk, chocolate
liqueur, toffee liqueur, chocolate
shavings, Crunchie bar
swizzle stick

Brain Damage

Half pint absinthe, vodka,
whisky, gin, Bacardi,
dash of amyl nitrate

Long Highland Mice Tea
Half pint of Highland whisky,
two white chocolate mice
to garnish

Hot Dog
Glass of brown ale, red ice pop
sticking out of the top for garnish

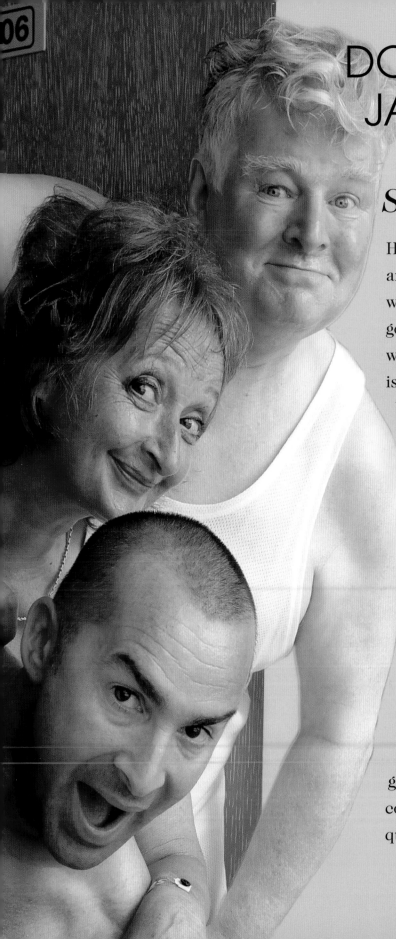

DONALD & JACQUELINE'S

Guide to a Swinging Holiday

Holaaaa! Jacqueline here. Donald and I have been asked to say a few words about making your holiday go with a 'swing', if you know what I mean. Now I know there is a chance that kiddies might be reading this book so we're going to cover the subject very lightly; if you want something a bit more in-depth and probing (I know I usually do) why not pre-order the first in our series of soon to be published self help books starting with, 'Donald & Jacqueline's Guide to a Happy Marriage' (see ad at the end of this book). Donald assures me it's great value for money, very thick and heavy and once you get it in your hands you'll keep coming back for more. (The book's quite good as well apparently.)

♂ Jacqueline and I have been holidaying on the Costa Blanca for some years now and each time we go away we seem to manage to "hook up" with several like-minded couples, sometimes pre-arranged, sometimes on the spur of the moment.

♀ I tend to enjoy the more impromptu meetings, much more fun. If we think we are in the company of like-minded individuals I'll generally say something like, "Donald and I are just going for a siesta. If anyone wants to join us you're more than welcome." I then follow this up with, "Well I say a siesta, it'll be more of a slumber party." And then, "Well I say slumber party, it'll be more of a bunk up." And finally, "Well, I say a bunk up, it'll be more of a…" Usually by this point people have either rolled up their towel and stand grinning from ear to ear with their tongue hanging out or have already left looking a bit peaky. Donald, however, likes to go for a slightly more direct approach.

WELL I SAY SLUMBER PARTY, IT'LL BE MORE OF A BUNK UP

♂ Oh indeed. Nothing ventured nothing gained I always say. I tend to come down to breakfast and test the waters by saying, "Hallo! Good to know you, my name's Donald Stewart, this is the wife Jacqueline, no reasonable offer refused!" If I think that comment went down well I tend to follow up with something a little more fruity such as, "Don't worry about Jacqueline standing up, her back end took a bit of a battering last night and she tends to smart a little on the hard plastic chairs."

♀ Donald once said that when we were visiting a friend of ours in pantomime while holidaying in Cleethorpes. Our friend Gay Derek is a semi professional actor and always plays "Dame" every year in theatres up and down the country. We were introduced to the stars of the show and although I can't possibly name who this husband and wife showbiz couple are I can reveal we stayed the night at their B&B digs and enjoyed a magical evening; they liked us, "not a lot" but they liked us!

♂ Although Cleethorpes was a bit of a one off, we find swinging holidays tend to be much better in the sun, a warm climate encouraging a free and easy state of mind. Benidorm is absolutely super for that and from late night video sessions on the dogging beach (you'll be amazed at the kind of people you bump into!) to the wonderful swinging clubs of the old town, there's always somewhere you can meet up with "like-minded" people.

♀ There's an absolutely fabulous swinging club in Albir, about 10 minutes drive from Benidorm (we tend not to take taxis, finding chumming up with someone who's hired a car for their holiday much more cost effective). Swingers' clubs are usually hidden away off the beaten track but just do a little internet search and you'll soon see pictures of Clive and Willamina hosting on a Tuesday and Wednesday night. Or if you happen to be passing at the weekend, their weekly "Bottom's Up" event on a Saturday night is an absolute hoot! Donald loves a long session at Clive and Willie's because there's a gorgeous fish and chip shop 2 minutes walk (stagger) from their back entrance and Donald doesn't feel he's had a good night out unless he ends the evening with a battered sausage.

♂ Don't forget the extremely useful classified advertisements in local papers too. We tend to pop a few lines in the free ads "personal" section to coincide with our two weeks in the sun. Be creative with your ad, use a little artistic licence, remember you'll only catch a whopper if you have juicy bait! Our last ad in the *Costa Blanca Snooze* read as follows: "Red hot couple: Him – late forties, classic swimmer's build, own hair and teeth, can be very passive with the right, sensitive kind of chap. Her: Hour glass figure, absolute stunner, Miss Billingham 1963, seek broadminded couples and singles for like-minded fun and frolics." Unfortunately there was a slight misprint and the ad read "Miss Bilious 1963" but we got a fair number of replies and ended up in a lovely three-way session with Horace, a retired glass blower from Rimswell. He was quite elderly and chronically asthmatic but with several comfort breaks per hour and his late wife's prosthetic leg propping open the window in his two-berth caravan we all got along famously.

♀ So basically what we're saying is "Nothing ventured, nothing gained." If you don't have the confidence to approach anyone or strike up a conversation, why not just read a sexy novel and see if anyone comments, I find *Lady Chatterley's Lover* does well or anything by Alan Titmarsh.

♂ Good luck with your swinging holiday and remember, if you have no joy meeting the right kind of people you can always take a break in Benidorm, last week in August, first week in September; you'll be guaranteed at least two people around the Solana pool who will be very accommodating, won't they, Jacqueline?

♀ Ooooooooh Yes!

SIGN OF THE TIMES

Struggling with the lingo? No worries, you've come to the right place. Learning a foreign language can take up so much precious time, especially when there is all-inclusive alcohol to consume and unlimited buffets to trough. You don't need a language to get by in Spain – the signs are there, and here's how to read them!

Just TAKE it!

GRATIS

Possibly the most important sign you will see on your holiday. It means whatever is within three feet of this sign is FREE. Don't ask, don't queue, just TAKE! Get it while you can – just like the toros in the Benidorm Bull Ring, you never know when they are gonna start charging!

Lift Roulette

You'll find this handy sign in most lifts in many hotels. It tells you the maximum capacity of the lift in both weight and estimated number of people. The problem is the sign was not made for the all-inclusive market. Yes, 450kg is equal to six people on a Club Med holiday but if your fortnight's holiday cost less than £200 per person chances are you're sharing a hotel with a bunch of wobbling lard arses that would leave Dr Christian open mouthed. You could of course go for the jovial approach asking your lift buddies directly, "All right pal, you're packing some beef, how many pounds are you pushing?" or "Christ love, I bet you've flattened some grass in your time, what are you? 15 stone?". There are so many variables to this (some involving hospitalisation, so make sure you have your European Healthcare Insurance Card to hand) that it's best to use this handy rule of thumb: 6 persons = 2 all inclusive. So if your lift carries 12 people how many Mr Blobbies should be getting in? Hm … We didn't say this was easy. Probably best to take the stairs – let's face it, you could do with the exercise.

450 KG
6 PERS.

CE
0099

RAE: 2330

MONTES TALLON, S/A

Piss-in-a-pool

PISCINA POOL

Another important sign. Not all pools are the type you can piss in. Many hotels insist you get out and walk to the toilet to have a waz (we know, crazy! Are you supposed to be on holiday or not?!). Make sure you only have a slash in the appropriate pool (look for the sign above) and remember, doing it off the diving board is just plain rude.

Salad!

This may sound strange but your body can only take so many unlimited buffets, burgers, sausages, chips, black pudding, ice cream, lollies and alcohol. Sometimes your body will start to crave for something called "salad". It's not nice but when you get to about day 6 of your fortnight's holiday you won't be able to go to the loo and your vision will be slightly impaired. This is your body crying out for "salad". Many hotels have tables of salad on standby for these such occasions, so look out for the sign above. Don't go mad, just have a few lettuce leaves and a bit of tomato (ketchup doesn't count) until you feel your heart begin to maintain a regular pulse.

Running of The Bulls

This is a sign you will only find in certain parts of Spain. It is usually spray painted on pavements or walls (as it is here) along the route for the "Running of The Bulls" or "Encierro" as it is sometimes known. This is a fiesta that involves the locals (and stupid tourists) running through the streets in front of an angry group or "bevy" of bulls (sometimes up to a dozen). At certain points in the route the action can get a little sedate so spectators are encouraged to push various objects/people into the path of the oncoming bovine traffic. As you can see from the sign, they don't take any prisoners, it's every man (or child) for himself so if you see this sign and can hear the sound of clattering hooves, best duck into the nearest karaoke bar and give them your best rendition of Tommy Steele's "Little White Bull." It certainly beats getting flattened by one!

INCENDIO!

This curious sign is often found in a small red box on the wall of a hotel or apartment block. This, again, is another crazy Spanish custom which will have you and your mates crying with laughter. The game of "Incendio" is best played in the middle of the night or very early in the morning (say 4 or 5 a.m.); first push the sign where indicated and wait for a loud alarm to sound – you're ready to play INCENDIO! As the ear-piercing alarm reverberates around the hotel you will find most guests run from their rooms shouting and screaming; join in with the shouting, it's all part of the fun! Some people will carry belongings with them, others (often the old and infirm) will be empty handed. The basic rule of INCENDIO is whatever you leave behind in your room/apartment is yours for the taking ("incendio" is Catilan for "free-for-all"). It's a bit like "Cabbages & Kings" in 1970s kids' favourite *Crackerjack*; carry as much as you can (clothes, towels, purses, cameras, etc) from the unoccupied rooms but if you drop anything it stays on the floor! Take your booty to your room, put it somewhere safe then join the rest of the players outside and wait for the game to end (the alarm will stop ringing). Have great fun playing INCENDIO and remember, we know this game sounds pretty implausible but this is a nation that runs down narrow streets being chased by angry bulls for a national pastime!

"MICHAEL BUBLÉ,
I WOULDN'T KICK
THAT ONE OUT IF IT
CRAWLED IN"

Janice

Full name:
Janice Garvey.

Place & date of birth:
Oldham.

Occupation:
Work in a Tanning Shop.

Favourite holiday destination & why?
Benidorm, it's simply the best (better than all the rest).

Favourite food?
Meat plate pie, or salad if I'm being good.

Favourite type of music?
Love all sorts. Michael Bublé (I wouldn't kick that one out if it crawled in).

Which TV shows do you watch?
I love me soaps!

Do you have a role model?
I used to have a Girls World when I was a kid. You know, the one where you pulled her hair out of the top. Is that what you mean?

If you had to rate yourself 1–10 in attractiveness, how would you score?
I don't know. Do you mean could I fancy meself? I'm not into all that carry on, I think you need to speak to Donald and whatsherface.

What has been your greatest accomplishment in life?
Raising two brilliant kids and having a gorgeous grandchild.
I'm hoping for more!

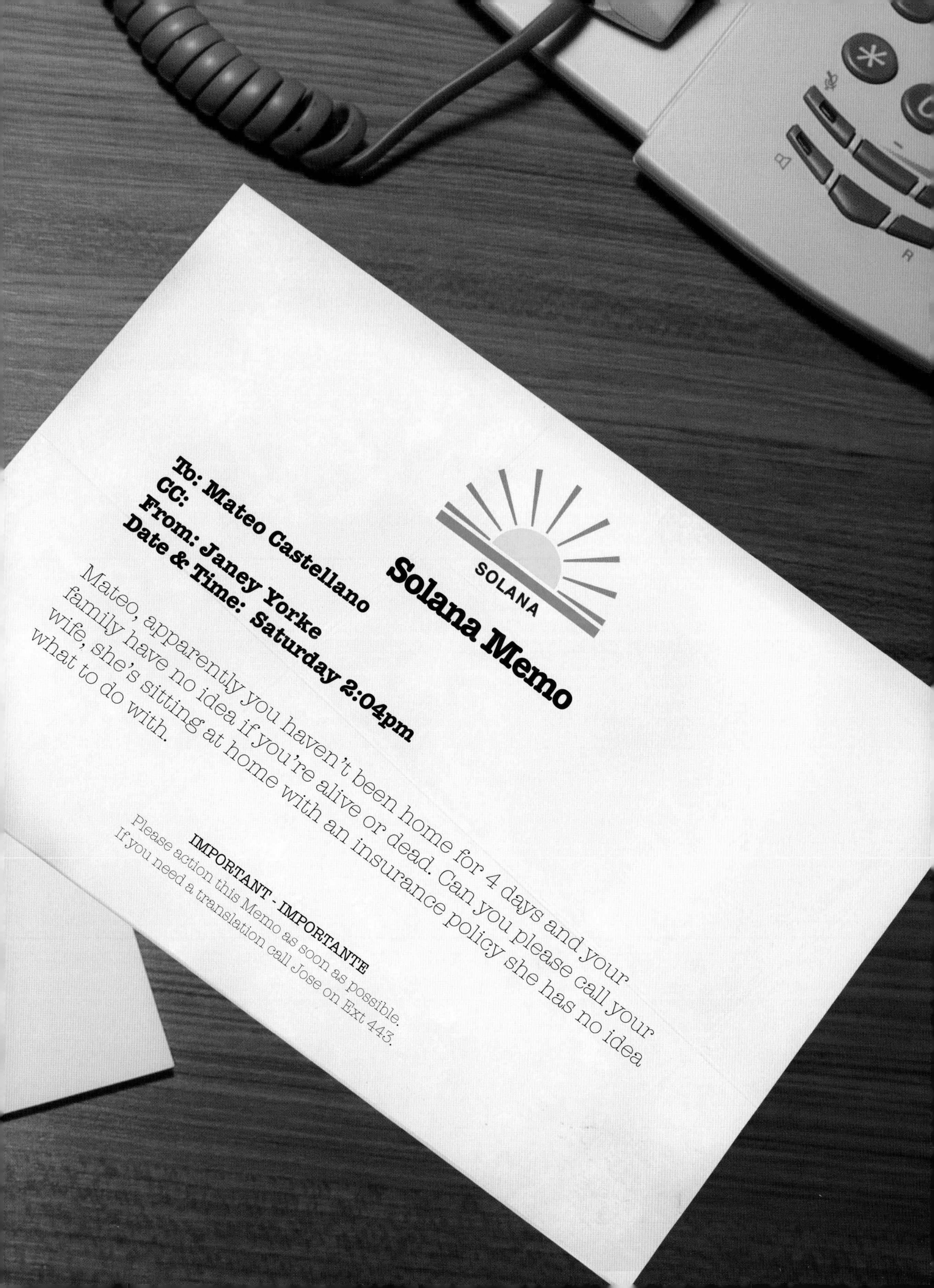

Solana Memo

To: Mateo Castellano
CC:
From: Janey Yorke
Date & Time: Saturday 2:04pm

Mateo, apparently you haven't been home for 4 days and your family have no idea if you're alive or dead. Can you please call your wife, she's sitting at home with an insurance policy she has no idea what to do with.

IMPORTANT - IMPORTANTE
Please action this Memo as soon as possible.
If you need a translation call Jose on Ext 443.

HOLIDAY *FASHION*

I was so lucky to be married to possibly the most elegant, chic, sophisticated and snappy dresser ever to have strolled the Levante prom. Mel Harvey was nothing less than a fashion icon and it's my pleasure to pass on some hints and tips to help you make the most of the contents of your suitcase and turn your vacation vestments into holiday haute couture!

ACCESSORISE!

People often would say my Mel looked a million dollars ("all in loose change" my son in law Mick used to add to that, cheeky bastard) and the secret of this was his natural ability to accessorise! Going to throw away an old pair of crimplene trousers because they are out of date and make your legs sweat? Cut the length in half, just above the knee, add a fancy belt and hey presto, you have a natty pair of smart/casual shorts that would be acceptable either at the beach or a very informal dinner dance that has no air conditioning. Another one of Mel's sayings was "If you want to get ahead, get a hat!" A hat not only can denote an air of authority but also a sense of humour. Only have room in your case for one hat? Fear not, wearing a hat several different ways can suit more than one occasion. Wearing a hat at a jaunty angle says, "I'm up for fun", wearing a hat on the back of your head lets people know you are approachable, wearing it low with the brim covering your face on the other hand says, "I'm having a nap – don't disturb!" There is one way of wearing a hat which is wrong and that's back to front. I've seen young kids walking around with all manner of hats on the wrong way round, American baseball caps, Greek fisherman's hats, flat caps; I've no idea who's told these young lads and lasses they look good but take it from me, we had a 13 year old boy in my school in the early fifties who wore his hat the wrong way round, he also had his legs in callipers, a patch on one eye of his glasses and told people he was a spy.

DRESSING FOR BREAKFAST

Dining on holiday can be great fun. Mel and I would always make an effort of an evening but don't forget nobody wants to sit next to a scruffy, unwashed toe-rag first thing in a morning. First of all, vests are a no-no while people are eating. An unlimited buffet can often attract the fat, greedy type who understandably have difficulty finding clothes to fit them. This is no excuse for a 22 stone man to have his tits out at breakfast. How would you like it if I did the same? No, I thought not. A short sleeved shirt is perfectly acceptable, a t-shirt if you must but please, NO comedy slogans. You may think it's hilarious to have "cover me with chocolate and throw me to the lesbians" emblazoned on your chest at nine o'clock in the morning but personally that's an image I can live without.

THESE BOOTS WERE MADE FOR WALKING

My Mel suffered terribly with his feet (and his back, his knees, his breathing and eyesight) but he always had the decency to wear the appropriate footwear to match the occasion. Nobody is saying you shouldn't wear flip flops on holiday but make an effort. Plastic is not a material that goes well next to bare feet, especially when heat is involved. The last thing you want is your dirty old trotters sweating in something manmade and that includes "leatherette" (a word to

"FASHION FADES, STYLE IS ETERNAL" SO SAID YVES SAINT LAURENT AND SHE SHOULD KNOW.

the wise, that's just another name for plastic). And do you really want to be standing on the side of the pool, your feet covered in boils? No, I thought not. Also, "Buy cheap, buy twice" is something my husband used to say and you could accuse him of several things but he certainly never bought cheap; well, not in clothing anyway (he once bought a rip-off bottle of Malibu called Balimu which gave us the shits for 3 nights running but that's another story).

IN THE SWIM

Now, this subject is slightly controversial. I always thought a good pair of baggy shorts were the order of the day when swimming or lounging in the pool area of your hotel but Mel being the ground-breaking visionary he was, once again, made me reassess my values. I always thought a thong was a ditty with a lisp. But no, a thong is a sophisticated, eye-catching, avant-garde item of swimwear which is a must-have accessory for all holiday fashionistas who happen to be in tip top physical shape. Note that last and very important point, "tip top physical shape"; a thong is not an item of clothing for the fat or the very thin. My Mel had the body of a Greek god and could carry off just about any item of clothing but if you're a skinny Minnie or a blubbering gut bucket a thong is going to do you no favours at all. In fact if you're a big fat walloper you might have trouble retrieving said thong after a long day baking in the sun. I've seen Mr Blobby look-alikes leaning against the poolside shower cubicles trying to tease arse chewed material out of the crack of their sweaty cheeks while women and children run screaming thinking the Martians have landed. Also, on the subject of whales, I have a message for gentlemen who happen to

have the misfortune of owning a pair of sweaty, hairy, man boobs or "moobs" as I believe they are called. (Well, I say the misfortune, if indeed having no will power and an aversion to physical exercise is a misfortune and not a choice.) When leaving the pool please put some clothes on as soon as possible. But even when fully clothed, when making your way over to the unlimited buffet on the strike of twelve, even though running there is the only exercise you ever take, try and keep it to a dignified stroll. There's enough food for everyone and there's nothing worse than having to explain to the kiddies why that big, fat, hyperventilating, bearded woman isn't wearing a bra.

DRESS TO IMPRESS

So what is my final word on holiday fashion? STYLE. You don't need a fortune to be a natty dresser. I was so lucky to have known my wonderful husband Mel and in the all too short time we spent together on this earth we certainly had our financial ups and downs; but no matter how rich or poor we were my Mel always stood out from the crowd; he had STYLE. I used to have a rich aunt who was a landlord with many houses (not that we ever got a whiff of her money, tight fisted old cow) and she always said, "I may buy cheap doors but I've always have fabulous knockers". And so we learn the lesson, your shirt and slacks may be Primark but push the boat out on a snazzy belt and you'll always look the part. "Fashion fades, style is eternal":

so said Yves Saint Laurent and she should know, she's been in the business long enough (mind you, I'm not surprised she's done well for herself, £31 for a pot of moisturiser ...). So here's to my Mel, a fashion icon the like of which we may never see again. Whether on a karaoke stage in a sash waisted, polyester pirate blouson, on a coach trip wearing casual slacks and a pastel cap or cutting a dash around the pool in an elasticated leopardskin thong, he always made me proud. Clothes maketh the man and there was no finer man than my dear Mel.

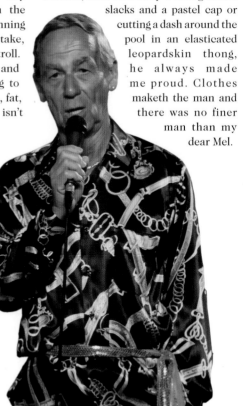

The Joy of Hot Pants

By **Kenneth du Beke**

If I could only give you three words of advice on what to pack for a summer holiday it would be Hot Pants, Hot Pants, Hot Pants. Hang on, that's six words; hotpants, hotpants, hotpants … No, that doesn't look right. Maybe it's hyphenated? Hot-pants? … Hm. ANYWAY, you see what I'm trying to say, dump those dull khaki shorts, throw away those three-quarter length trousers and put down those pedal pushers; pack light, pack small, pack sexy, PACK HOT PANTS! You only get one chance to make a first impression and when you first appear around that pool in the sizzling sun you need to let everyone know there's some fresh meat in town (well, fairly fresh).

The History of Hotpants

The hot pant was invented in the year 2000 by Dame Kylie Minogue when she wore a particularly fabulous pair of gold, ruched hot pants for her music video "Spinning Around". Now before you write in, YES, I know hot pants were around well before then but let's face it when HRH (Her Royal Hotpantsness) Kylie stepped out in those ass-hugging, shimmering shorties everyone who had gone before needn't have bothered.

Why Hot Pants?

You say "why hot pants?", I say, "WHY NOT?!" As in the words of the great Susan Boyle, "If you've got it, flaunt it" and let's face it, hot pants leave nothing to the imagination. Another reason to choose hot pants for the backbone of your summer wardrobe is they take up so little room. I don't mean on your person (although that's also a blessing), I mean in your luggage. I once went to Tenerife in 1990 with nothing but two vests, six pairs of hot pants and a catering pack of johnnies in a Netto carrier (of course coming back was even lighter, fifteen phone numbers and 800 Silk Cut, but that's another article). You don't need to be laden down with luggage for a belting break in the sun.

Short Shorts or Hot Pants?

Let's be absolutely clear on one thing, short shorts are NOT hot pants. I'm sick and tired of those who struggle into a pair of tiny shorts and claim they are working the hot pants look. WRONG! Hot pants need to look as if they've come out of an aerosol, they need to be at least 60% lycra and at least 30% wedged up your arse; anything less can simply not be described as hot pants!

Camel Toe

As long as there have been hot pants there has been camel toe; and it's not just a problem for the ladies. Male camel toe is a world-wide problem from Bali to Benidorm. If you are generous of thigh and not exactly hung like a Blackpool donkey a tight hot pant can often create the illusion that is male camel toe. I don't want to go into detail here but Playtex bras aren't the only underwear to lift and separate. So what is the solution? The solution, girlfriend, is staring you in the face (if you look hard enough). EMBRACE IT! Camel toe is part and parcel (or should that be package?) of wearing hot pants. Go with the flow, love your hot pants and love your camel toe.

To Enhance or Not To Enhance

Finally we come to the controversial subject of whether or not to artificially "enhance" your God given goods, your hot pants package, your lycra load. Personally I say embrace the camel toe, the alternative can have potentially devastating effects. I was once on a particularly cold holiday in Skegness in the summer of 1999 and the inclement weather was doing me no favours at all. I'd gone from camel toe to no toe and was getting some very admiring looks from a lady from Widnes called Pat who had a penchant for k d Lang and comfortable shoes, if you know what I mean. In a desperate attempt to save face I popped a frankfurter from breakfast down the front of my hot pants. All well and good until the afternoon when I'd had a few cocktails and didn't notice my Bavarian bratwurst had slowly edged its way down my thigh and was hanging out of my hot pants for all to see. I've been thrown out of Butlins before but my protestations of "What's your problem? Half the people here have been eating that for breakfast for the past week" made sure I got a lifetime ban.

My top 5 Hot Pants...

Take these 5 hot pants with you on holiday and have a look for every occasion.

CLASSIC PLAIN BLOCK HOT PANTS
Elegant and timeless, you can work this look anytime of the day or night. Understated but always HOT, choose a dark pair for breakfast (you don't want to be pulling focus from that breakfast sausage) and a more adventurous colour for around the pool. Your hot summer holiday just got hotter!

CAMOUFLAGE HOT PANTS
Great for a holiday hike or midnight manoeuvres although you'll hardly blend into the scenery with this mega-military look. Stand up straight and suck in that gut boy, as in the words of Status Quo, "You're in the army now!".

SEQUINDED HOT PANTS
The definitive disco look, these beauties are mainly worn after dark but can still be surprisingly versatile. Choose gaudy gold or racy red for Spanish nightclubs, but settle on a more restrained black or white option for state banquets. In saying this is an eveningwear only look, I once saw it pulled off around a pool (so to speak) in 2006 but that was a premiership footballer at a private beach party on Fire Island, oh Christiano, will we ever meet again?!

RUBBER HOT PANTS
Not for the hotter destination, I once lost about half a stone in sweat shimmying on a podium in a Egyptian nightclub in 1991 to Color Me Badd's "I Wanna Sex You Up". Also don't bother if your budget won't stretch to a high quality rubber. The last thing you want to do is rot your gusset and have an "under carriage fall out". Distressing for you but potentially traumatic for people dancing at eye level to your podium.

KYLIE RUCHED GOLD HOT PANTS
Wear these at your peril. HRH has already set the bar way too high for these legendary hot pants but if you genuinely feel you have the ass for them, then in the words of Messrs Michael & Ridgely (Young Guns) Go For It!

Health And Safety Incident Report

Incident Date: 7th October 2007
Incident time: Aprox 9pm
Incident Location: Neptune's evening
Incident Event: Karaoke
Person(s) involved: Mr Wank McAndrew
Injury sustained: Death

Summary of Incident:

I was taking the usual evening karaoke session, when Mr McAndrew, dressed in a tartan hat, orange wig, joke shop kilt and a t-shirt inviting people to "Cover me in chocolate and throw me to the lesbians" took to the stage and began to dance an improvised highland fling. I must say at this point, Mr McAndrew's improvised dance was considered by most to be hugely offensive, exposing a joke shop nylon penis to several patrons seated near the front of the stage. The intro of Mr McAndrew's chosen karaoke song played – "I'm Gonna Be (500 miles)" by The Proclaimers and Mr McAndrew grasped the microphone stand. This not only caused an electrical fault which temporarily shorted the lights in Neptune's but also resulted in the death of Mr McAndrew. The first to the stage were myself and Mr Castellanos (head barman) where the cause of the electrical fault was judged to be Mr McAndrew's nylon penis brushing against the mic stand. This along with his nylon Tam O'Shanter, nylon wig, and nylon kilt caused a build up of static electricity that surged uncontrollably once Mr McAndrew grabbed hold of the mic stand. At no point did Mr McAndrew's death interrupt the flow of the evening's entertainment and karaoke was resumed as the body was disposed of.

Signed:

Janey Mare.

Witnessed by:

Mateo

SOLANA

1

Did you spot the difference?

Answer on page 152

The Holiday Gu

BY MADGE HARVEY

Whether you're waking up in a Costa Blanca casa or a Cleethorpes caravan, fumbling around on that bedside table and sparking up a fag in the dark before you open your eyes is one of the true great pleasures in life. I've been smoking 40 cigarettes a day since I was twelve years old and I'm living proof that the "evil weed" is anything but. Sadly, the world is full of interfering do-gooders and most of Europe is now in the stranglehold of a ludicrous smoking ban and these continental cloth heads seem to think they should tell us how to live our lives.

1ST JULY 2007 WAS A DARK DAY FOR ME (even though it was middle of summer), the UK smoking ban was like someone cutting off my oxygen supply. If it wasn't bad enough not being able to have a fag on the top deck of the bus while heading into town or in the back of the cinema we now had the ultimate indignity: no smoking in pubs. Now let's get one thing straight, an alcoholic drink without a cigarette is like a baby without a dummy and while the veggie chomping, soap dodging, "right on" moaning bastards would be up in arms about the baby's "human rights" to a dummy, what about our human rights for a nice Silk Cut 100 with a vodka and orange?

Well, at least there was Spain. Just because the idiots in charge of the UK wanted a smoking ban they couldn't ruin our holidays as well ... That delicious first waft of stale smoke hanging in the air as I scootered into Neptune's used to be bloody gorgeous. I'd be like a Bisto kid, eyes half closed, nose in the air, sniffing out the different pockets of nicotined fog; a bit of Berkeley Red here, Marlboro Lights over there, maybe a fruity puff of menthol from a kiddie with their first cheeky pack of 10 Consulate ... mmmmm, delicious. Well, no more my friends, no more. Those nasty, evil, twisting Spanish bastards have done it again. You get off a 2½ hour fag free flight, practically climbing the walls and what happens, you get offloaded into Alicante airport where there is NO SMOKING.

NO SMOKING. WHAT'S THE FUCKING POINT OF BEING ON HOLIDAY???!!!!

You get onto a transfer coach to Benidorm, another 50 minutes of NO SMOKING. You get to the hotel, you just want to sit in a nice foam backed wicker chair in reception and relax but you can't because there's NO SMOKING. You go out to Neptune's that night and you want to warm up your throat for an evening of karaoke but you can't because there's NO SMOKING. Pardon my French but WHAT'S THE FUCKING POINT OF BEING ON HOLIDAY???!!!!

Sorry about that but you can see my point. And another thing, if they don't want us to smoke, why do they sell them so cheap?!!

ide to Smoking

TELL THEM TO SHOVE IT UP THEIR ARSES!

It's political correctness gone mad. Well, this is my guide to smoking on holiday and you'll be pleased to read it's very short and very simple. TELL THEM TO SHOVE IT UP THEIR ARSES! The Spanish authorities tried three times to stop their people smoking and each time the Spaniards did what they're best at, they were pig ignorant. They flatly refused, carried on smoking in bars, kept on puffing in restaurants and told the government to stick it up their Spanish arses. Well the latest ban came into force on 2nd January 2011, and the Spaniards have finally been broken and like a naughty dog who's just dropped the worst cabbage fart in history, they've been sent outside with their tails between their collective legs … and they've gone.

Well I'm here to say UP THE REVOLUTION! Let's do what we did in 1939 and all pull together and make a difference! (All right, I was only two in 1939 but I remember lying in me pram in Baddlescroft Ex-Servicemen's Club sucking up air, thick with a heady cocktail of Park Drive and No.6 Tipped thinking, "Nobody's taking this away from me!"). What's the worst that could happen? They can't throw us all in jail can they? (Can they??!!) If we just show a bit of solidarity and the kind of spirit that used to make Britain great. Think of all the times the people of Britain have pulled together, we've always made a difference. What about that time all them prisoners got on top of the roof at Strangeways? Twenty-five days they were up there, nobody told them what to do (well, until day twenty-six when they all went back into the prison but you get my drift). Next time you're sitting in a bar in Benidorm or a café in the Canaries, get 20 of your favourite fags out and spark up with pride. If they take us they'll take us together! All for one and one for all! As the President of the United States keeps saying (I can never remember his name, black fella, tall, married to Oprah Winfrey … oh what is it?! Sounds like Copacabana … you know who I mean) – Yes we can! Yes we can!

Yes we can!

Spanish Pick and Mix

KARAOKE
FUNERAL

Funerals can be a morbid affair, get the ageing relatives going with a wake to remember.

1. GOING UNDERGROUND – *The Jam* *(Burials)*
2. BURN BABY BURN DISCO INFERNO – *The Trammps (Cremations)*
3. THE DRUGS DON'T WORK – *The Verve (Non Treatable Illnesses)*
4. YOU RAISE ME UP – *Boyzone (Exhumations)*
5. HANGING AROUND – *The Stranglers (Suicides)*
6. I COULDN'T SLEEP A WINK – *Frank Sinatra (Accidental Overdose Of Sleeping Tablets)*
7. THE BEST IS YET TO COME – *Frank Sinatra (Reincarnation Believers)*
8. OUT OF MY HEAD – *Black Eyed Peas (Dementia)*
9. MY HEART WILL GO ON – *Celine Dionne (Organ Donors)*
10. I'VE GOT MY LOVE TO KEEP ME WARM – *Eartha Kitt (Double Burials)*

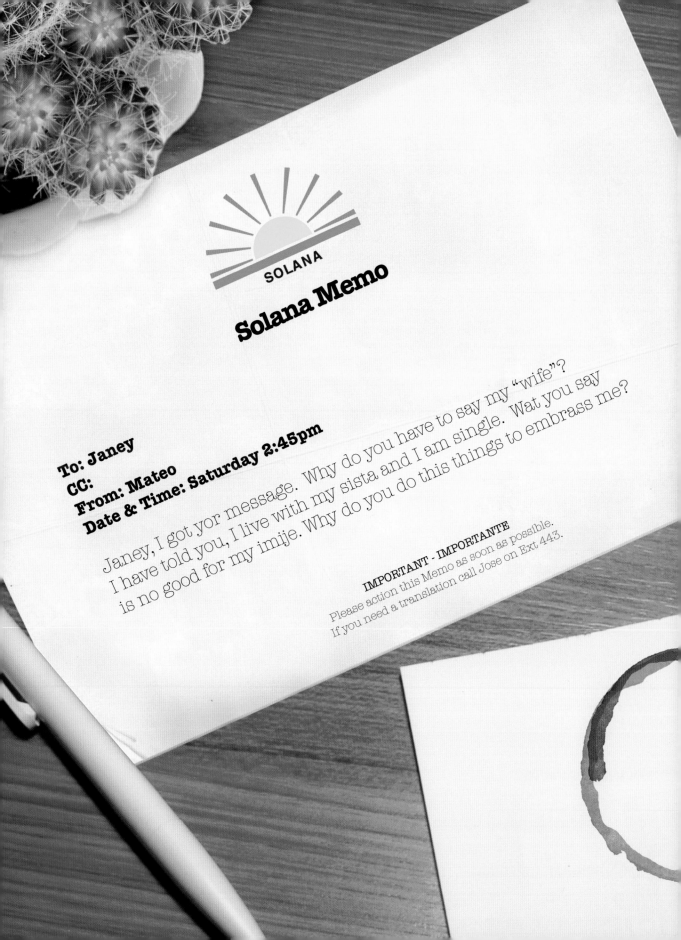

SOLANA

Solana Memo

To: Janey
CC:
From: Mateo
Date & Time: Saturday 2:45pm

Janey, I got yor message. Why do you have to say my "wife"? I have told you, I live with my sista and I am single. Wat you say is no good for my imije. Why do you do this things to embrass me?

IMPORTANT - IMPORTANTE
Please action this Memo as soon as possible.
If you need a translation call Jose on Ext 443.

Psychic Readings by
ROMANY JOE
Psychic to the stars!

Hawaiian Function Room every Wednesday afternoon 11 a.m.

Join Joe on an incredible journey through his Romany family history from the fish docks of Hull to the bright lights of Benidorm, highlighting his brief career as a cabaret singer and the rare psychic gifts that have been passed on to him from previous generations.

This bum-numbing talk will end (eventually) with the opportunity for you to have your own personal psychic reading with Joe for the discounted price of €10.

"You couldn't predict the outcome of a one horse race"
Lester Piggott

"Stop using my photo outside your caravan, I've never met you"
Paul O'Grady

"How you knew I came from Jamaican parents I'll never know"
Lenny Henry

"A gifted and wonderful man"
Derek Acorah

SOLANA
www.solanabenidorm.com

Janice Garvey's
GUIDE TO HOLIDAY EATING

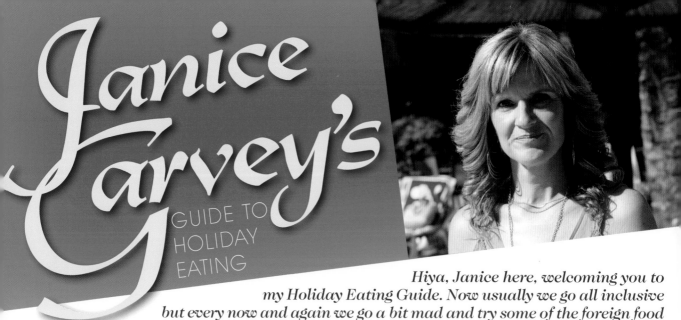

Hiya, Janice here, welcoming you to my Holiday Eating Guide. Now usually we go all inclusive but every now and again we go a bit mad and try some of the foreign food that you can get while on your holidays. I know most people think local food on holiday is to be avoided at all costs but nothing ventured nothing gained, that's what I say. Here we go.

PAELLA

Now this is an interesting one. First of all you might think it is special fried rice with a bit of extra swag on top but no, take a closer look. Most of that shite resting on top of that rice is completely inedible. Mussels in shells (if you can't eat it why put it on the plate?!), squid (more on that later!) and prawns; now I know what you're going to say, what's wrong with prawns?? Nothing when they're on a bed of lettuce in a nice marie rose sauce (tommy sauce and mayonnaise!) but these prawns have still got their eyes and they're looking up at you! 'Nuff said!

SQUID

Now just wait 'til you hear about this one! When I was a kid me and me sister Valda went to the cinema to see a film which I think was called *20,000 Leagues Under The Sea*. In this film (quite good as I remember) there is a giant octopus, have you seen it? You might still be able to get it on DVD; anyway, squid is basically a tiny version of that octopus! I know, UNBELIEVABLE! And they don't even chop it up or liquidize it or anything, they leave it there on your plate with all it's long, rubbery legs (called testicles) waving in the air. You have been warned!

CALAMARI
THESE ARE NOT, REPEAT, NOT ONION RINGS!
You only make that mistake once!

HUMOUS

Now this is bloody lovely. It's a bit like toast toppers (do you remember them?) or some kind of sandwich spread that you dip that nice kebab bread into. Do be warned though, if you go to one of them hippy type places that sell brown rice (who eats BROWN rice?!) and tofu they might try and serve the humous with that horrible pebble dashed bread (also called "wholemeal"). Forget it, tastes like bloody cardboard.

CROQUETAS DE JAMON

Don't worry about this one, I know written down it looks like a bad hand at Scrabble but they are basically potato crockets. And before you say it, no, there's no ham in it, 'jamon' means there are bits of 'jam on it'. Although the jam is not on it, it's inside it but obviously some things get lost in translation. Just so you know, despite them having jam in them they are not sweet, they are savoury, the jam tastes a bit like pork. I'm not selling these very well am I? Just do yourself a favour and get some ordered, oh did I mention they are deep fried? Now you're interested aren't you?!

TARAMASALATA

OK, this one is a bit of a split decision. I didn't mind the look of this at first because it seemed to be just like humous. Plus it's the same lovely pink as a top I bought in Benidorm outdoor market a few years ago. But then I found out that it's basically whipped fish. And not any old fish but that cod roe stuff that me Dad used to eat. In saying that our Michael loves it so I'd say give it a go but just remember, you're eating whipped fish.

DONALD & JACQUELINE'S

Holiday Wordsearch 2

LUGGAGE	PING PONG	SHOTS	BUDGET
EUROS	COCKTAILS	KARAOKE	TREE
BREAKFAST	SWIM	RESORT	SUNBED
ISLAND	TRANSFER	BOOK	LATE
ARRIVALS	FLYING	CABARET	TICKET

D	S	T	R	O	S	E	R	F	U	B	C	O	C	K
E	W	R	S	A	G	C	T	K	A	R	A	O	K	E
B	I	E	T	A	L	I	K	R	M	E	B	C	R	P
N	M	E	G	N	C	C	R	U	Z	A	U	O	E	A
U	L	G	J	K	O	I	B	O	O	K	M	C	F	N
S	U	G	E	C	V	M	S	I	J	F	M	K	S	T
L	N	T	N	A	S	H	I	T	B	A	L	N	N	I
T	I	D	L	O	S	D	N	A	L	S	I	U	A	E
I	P	S	R	F	P	T	A	W	T	T	C	P	R	S
T	S	U	L	E	I	G	K	T	S	G	K	S	T	T
S	E	W	A	L	L	A	N	A	N	A	L	E	C	E
S	W	A	V	T	I	T	N	I	N	U	G	S	O	R
T	A	N	I	C	C	U	Y	U	P	D	K	N	C	A
O	N	K	R	H	P	L	P	U	U	C	R	A	K	B
H	K	B	R	S	F	S	S	B	O	E	W	R	S	A
S	L	I	A	T	K	C	O	C	S	T	I	T	S	C

I'd like the steak, rare, just a faint pulse.
Quisiera el filete, raro, apenas un pulso débil.

I think beguiling is the word that springs to mind.
Pienso que que seduce es la palabra esa las primaveras a importar.

Does the all you can eat buffet include pudding?
¿Hace el todo lo que usted puede comer la comida fría incluyen el pudín?

I couldn't eat another thing; do you fancy a lolly?
No podría comer otra cosa; ¿usted desea un polo?

When it comes to sloppy seconds I don't mind bringing up the rear
Cuando viene a los segundos descuidados yo no importe el sacar a colación de a parte posterior.

Do you have any cheesy nibbles?
¿Usted tiene nibbles caseosos?

Your face or mine?
¿Su cara o mina?

Did you know you can get a pack of sausages for 16 pence?
¿Usted le conocía puede conseguir un paquete de las salchichas para 16 peniques?

That's the trouble with buffets, they're very more-ish.
Ése es el problema con las comidas frías, ellos es muy apetitoso.

Do you want to go halves on a pineapple fritter?
¿Usted quiere ir las mitades en un buñuelo de la piña?

Kenneth

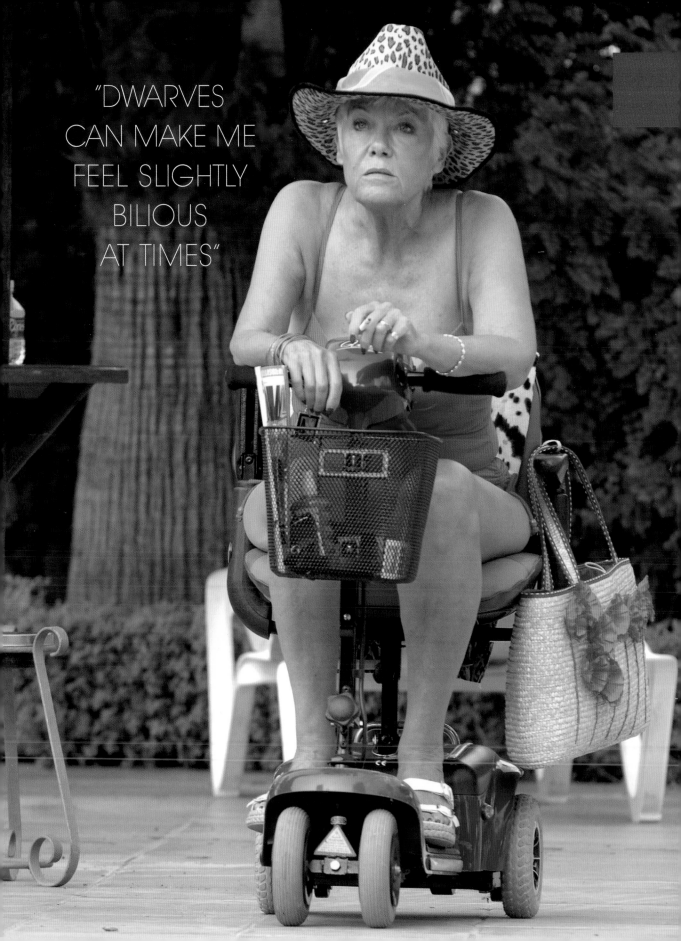

"DWARVES CAN MAKE ME FEEL SLIGHTLY BILIOUS AT TIMES"

Sylvia

Full name:
You can call me Sylvia.

Place & date of birth:
Place, London, date, don't be so bleeding rude.

Occupation:
I have decided to take early retirement.

Favourite holiday destination & why?
Anywhere but Benidorm, went once, full of bloody nutcases.

Favourite food?
I like the finer things in life.

Favourite type of music?
My beautiful daughter Kelly bought me that album by "Subo". Not a bad singing voice for a wrestler.

Which TV shows do you watch?
I used to love that show with the little fella who used to shout, "The plane, the plane". Was it *Fantasy Island*? Strange for me because dwarves can make me feel slightly bilious at times.

Do you have a role model?
Baroness Thatcher.

If you had to rate yourself 1–10 in attractiveness, how would you score?
I'm like Bo Derek, a 10.

What has been your greatest accomplishment in life?
Preventing my daughter marrying some dodgy Spanish waiter in a horrible all inclusive she was working in. Greasy baaaastard.

HAVE YOU SEEN
THIS WOMAN?

Please contact Mel Harvey on Benidorm
+ 34 0776 36322

REWARD OFFERED

MIDDLESBROUGH SWINGERS ASSOCIATION
COUNCIL VOTING FORM

The MSA or Middlesbrough Swingers' Association was founded in 1962 by Roger Bainbridge (now Baroness Bainbridge of Ashby de la Zouch) with only three members (Roger, his then wife Miriam and their Spanish lodger Manny Sanchez), but is now the oldest swingers' association in the UK with some 200 members. The MSA is part of the infamous 'Golden Ring', an elite membership of six Swingers' Associations which all other swingers' associations model themselves on.

The MSA members are once again running for council and they need your support! The Middlesbrough Swingers' Association take election to council membership very seriously, so please, only vote for members you have slept with.

BENNY SMALLCOCK

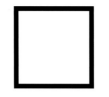

As a relatively new member you may think twice about voting for me but I can assure you I had been serving on council for the Derbyshire Swingers' Association for almost ten years before a job change and an unfortunate police prosecution forced me to move into the MSA catchment area. I come from a long line of swingers, my great grandather being Norris Smallcock, a key witness in the Oscar Wilde trial of 1895. I look forward to meeting members in the next meeting (I think it's Donald & Jacqueline Stewart's Annual Sauna Sizzle) and show you how my given surname is HUGELY ironic.

MARIANNE CULVERHOUSE

At 91 I am the oldest serving member on council. I may be in my nineties but I still go like a steam train. Vote for experience, vote Culverhouse.

DONALD STEWART

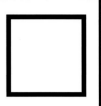

I have been a council member now for 14 years. I organised our MSA Christmas Jamboree to Benidorm and our infamous Brighton Blow-Out in 2008. Also, since the collapse of the Nardinis hot tub in September of last year Jacqueline and I will continue hosting our fortnightly 'Lube Party' for as long as the indoor paddling pool holds up. I look forward to you giving it to me (the vote I mean!).

COSTAS NICOLAU

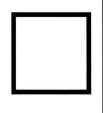

Hallo my friends, Costas here standing for council for the first time since joining the MSA in 2006. If voted to council I promise to give 10% discount on all take away food and fizzy drinks from my kebab shop "Hot Meat" which is conveniently situated opposite the dogging car park on Quimby Lane. Also full use of my wife on Monday nights after early closing.

DONNA MILLHOUSE

Hey guys and gals, Big Donna here asking for your votes once again to have some BBW (Big Beautiful Woman) representation on the council. As you know I abandoned my attempt at forming a 'XXL Swingers' Association' for the larger proportioned swinger due to technical difficulties. It's not that that we couldn't get enough fat swingers, we just couldn't find a meeting room that was big enough for us all to fit in. Vote for me – remember, thin may be in but fat's where it's at!

FRANCIS WAGTAIL

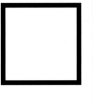

Hey guys, Franny here to say vote for me again and I'll make sure I serve you well (especially during S&M nights!). As many of you know I've had problems getting to all the meetings in the last few months due to hospitalisation but I can confirm the neck brace came off last week and I'm ready for action! Although do remember my new catchphrase, "Let go of my ears, I know what I'm doing!" x

DEREK MILLIGAN

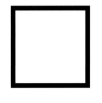

Hello Honky Tonks, Gay Derek here asking for your votes one last time before we emigrate to Thailand in 2013. Lenny and I have had a wonderful 10 years with the MSA and I've been assured by new member Jasper Nash that he will continue our annual Bottoms Up Evening in our honour. If voted to council for one last year I promise to leave my full collection of Anal Intruders to the MSA on my departure to sunnier climes (it's a bugger getting them through customs anyway). Love & kisses, Derek x

BARBARA AND ERIC DWYER

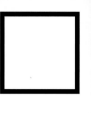

Hey fellow swingers, Eric and I are standing for council again. We feel it is so important that S&M practices are not ghettoised within the MSA. Come on people, don't drive us underground (although we don't mind being locked in a cellar!), we need a fair crack of the whip! I can assure you even though Eric is currently in hospital (again) he can undertake all council duties and attend all meetings either in person or via Skype. Mistress Barb Dwyer.

Sticky Vicky

A BENIDORM LEGEND

Dancer, magician, cabaret artiste, legend. Vicky Leyton, better known as Sticky Vicky, has been wowing Benidorm audiences with her "sexy magic show" for what seems like a lifetime. Born in Tenerife she came to Benidorm in the early eighties as a classically trained dancer but felt she needed a gimmick to make her act stand out from the rest.

Bringing magic bang up to date, she dispensed with the traditional magician's top hat and decided it would be much more of a talking point to make all of her props appear from the most magical place of all. She started off with simple props, two eggs, a hanky and a feather. As the act became more popular Vicky became more adventurous, including candles, light bulbs, a full English breakfast and at Christmas a fully illuminated Christmas tree (it's for the kiddies). Of course watching a woman in her late sixties pull more swag than an Argos catalogue out of her "auntie mary" might not be everyone's

cup of tea but audiences have voted with their feet and pack out bars and clubs several times a night to watch the legendary "Sticky Vicky" every time they

> "VICKY BECAME MORE ADVENTUROUS, INCLUDING CANDLES, LIGHT BULBS, A FULL ENGLISH BREAKFAST"

go to Benidorm. Although having no intentions of retiring, Vicky Leyton is safeguarding the tradition of "sexy magic" and has passed down the secrets of her magic box (quite literally) to her

daughter Demaria Leyton. In recent years the Benidorm cabaret circuit has spawned an impostor, a devious fake, a pretender to the "sexy magic" throne. This outrageous phoney, masquerading as the legend that is Sticky Vicky, using her name and cribbing her act is not the real deal. Accept NO imitations, see the original and the best, Vicky Leyton:

NIGHTMARE IN ⫽ THE SUN ⫽⫽ NIGHT...

ONE MAN'S CHILLING TALE OF ROBBERY AND INJUSTICE

A sad and too familiar tale

Going on holiday? Think you have adequate travel insurance? THINK AGAIN! This story of theft, pain and loss will make you go over your insurance policy again and again with a fine-tooth comb because nobody wants a NIGHTMARE IN THE SUN!

It was an ordinary day in Benidorm, Mr Hugh Janus was enjoying a family holiday, walking back to his rented timeshare villa to be reunited with his wife and two children after a sneaky couple of lunchtime pints when disaster struck.

What followed left Hugh Janus gaping in wonder ...

On passing The Jail Rock Bar in Calle Gerona Mr Janus was attacked by a naked thief. "It was more of a mental attack than a physical one," Mr Janus recalled. "He ran directly at me and I was terrified. All sorts of horrifying scenarios ran through my head, why was a naked man running towards me? I wasn't in the old town so I guessed he wasn't going to try and bum

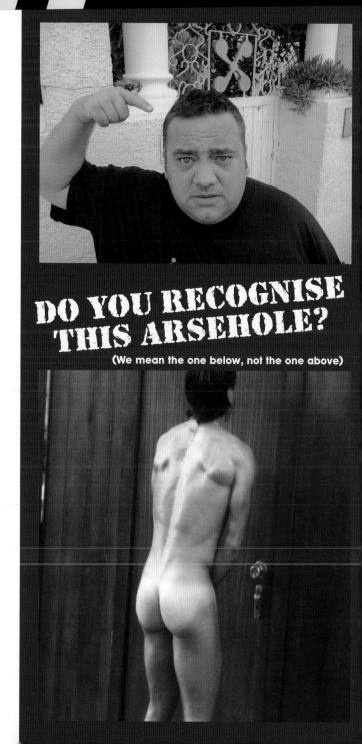

DO YOU RECOGNISE THIS ARSEHOLE?

(We mean the one below, not the one above)

THE SUN
MARE IN THE SUN -

me but as he lunged at me, panic stricken, I closed my eyes." When Mr Janus opened his eyes again a split second later he realised the nude attacker had made off with one of his prize possessions, his lucky hat. "I couldn't believe it, I'd had that hat six years. We had gone through so much together, I've even been completely arseholed in Café B until 4 and 5 in the morning and STILL not lost it (the hat I mean). I was once so drunk in my favourite karaoke bar, The Carousel, I staggered home leaving my son asleep in his buggy behind the bar but I didn't forget my hat. It's been my talisman, my juju, my lucky charm." Not wanting to give up without a fight Mr Janus took to his heels and ran after the butt-naked bandit in a vain attempt to be reunited with his filched fedora. The chase lasted an unbelievable three hours and involved the local police. "I'll say one thing for him, he was fast. I'm pretty sure the reason he could run faster than me was because he was naked, so he had no clothes weighing him down," said the 20 stone Mr Janus.

Despite local holiday makers coming forward with snapped pics of the event, the mystery naked nabber has yet to be identified. Do you recognise the naked man in the picture? Many people have bare faced cheek but bare arsed cheek is a new one even for Benidorm. A recent identity parade of disrobed derrières at the Benidorm police station resulted in nothing but a severe case of collective embarrassment.

Call Beni Crime Stoppers now on +34 099 91199.

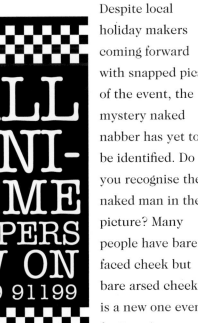

CALL BENI-CRIME STOPPERS NOW ON +34 099 91199

NOT IMPRESSED: Mr Janus was given a replacement hat after locals held a "yard of vodka" drinking competition and raised 6 euros. But the photo says it all.

CAUGHT IN THE ACT: A unsuspecting Hugh Janus goes about his business, calling a takeaway pizza to meet him when he gets home just as the culprit strikes.

ALL CRIED OUT: Mr Janus desperately searches online, and in vain, to find an exact replica of his original hat but it's all too much for him.

SOLANA

Lesley's Afternoon Bingo

Come and join Lesley, the lady with the biggest balls in Benidorm!

Join your host the lovely Lesley in the HAWAIIAN FUNCTION ROOM at 1 p.m. every Tuesday and Friday and play all star bingo!

- (25) **GREAT** atmosphere!

- (1) **FREE** Bingo Cocktail!

- (7) **PLAY** as many cards as you like!

- (39) **FREE** dabbers!

Single line, four corners or a full house, everyone's a winner at Lesley's Afternoon Bingo!*

*Please note not all prizes are exactly as described, no laptops can be won in Lesley's afternoon bingo.

www.solanabenidorm.com

Two hundred Berkley
Querido dosciento Berkley

Superkings please, darling.
Superkings carino por favor

Have you got a light?
¿Usted tiene fuego?

I need to charge my electric scooter.
Necesito cargar mi vespa eléctrica

Where is the local tanning shop?
¿Dónde es el departamento el broncear local?

Large vodka and orange please.
Vodka y naranja grandes por favor.

Oh, stick it up your arse.
Oh, pegúelo encima de su culo.

I know all about conspiracy theories, I once met Mohammed Al Fayed in a lift.
Sé todos sobre teorías de conspiración. Al una ves resuelto Fayed del Mohammed en una elevación.

If it's a boy she'll never walk again.
Si es un muchacho ella nunca recorrerá otra ves.

Shove it.
Empújelo.

Who the frigg's touché turtle?
¿Quién la tortuga del touché de los frigg?

Madge

Hola

My name is Mateo. You look beautiful this evening. I cannot remember the last time I saw a woman as delicious as you. You make me hungry. Not hungry to eat ham-booger, but hungry for your lips, for your arms, for your ... Oh Santa Maria. *(NOW CLOSE EYES AND MAKE A FACE LIKE YOU ARE TOUCHING YOURSELF, ALTHOUGH DO NOT, REPEAT, DO NOT.)*

The words on the left are an example of how to talk to ladies on holiday. It does not matter if you are on holiday yourself or if, like me, you work in a holiday resort. Women on holiday go crazy and will listen to these words and think you are in love with them. Of course when I meet a girl and tell her I am in love with her it is the truth. I may only be in love with her for a week, a night or maybe one hour but I am in love. Of course sometimes in a nightclub I might just kiss a girl, this time I am not in love, I am probably just drunk and want to have a quick feel before I go home.

Holiday Romance

Of course when you are in love with a girl on holiday it is sometimes necessary to fall out of love and get rid of her. This is important particularly when you have panicked and chosen a girl who is a little bit piggy in the face. I know the ancient English proverb "Every hole is a goal" can be true but some pig faced girls are difficult to get rid of when the next coachload of holiday makers arrive and there are some fit ones on it. The best way to get rid of your pig girl is to tell her she is too fat and make her cry. This may seem like a bad thing but you will only feel like a bad person while she is crying in front of you. As soon as she goes away you will feel better about yourself and be able to fall in love again with one of the fit girls who look better in a bikini and do not have an ass like a jelly. By the way, don't worry if the pig girl you are trying to lose is not fat, all girls think they are fat so my plan works OK for both.

Now I know some of you will be reading this and saying, "Mateo, the words you speak are wise and clever but I do not look like you, I do not have the body of a Greek god or the face of a film star." I know, but all you have to do is lower your standards a little. But even an ugly guy can still get a girl if you look after your body. Go to the gym every day – I have a great work out partner, he is called Ricky, he is 25 and from Brazil. We met in my local gym, he is a good looking guy and has great abs and legs. Ricky works as a dancer in the old town of Benidorm. I make fun of him because he has to dance on a little stage in a nightclub wearing gold underwear that go right up his ass. There are no girls in the club where Ricky works but we don't mind because the guys are cool and many of them go to our gym anyway so they are cool and one of them cuts his hair for free. So follow my advice and like Ricky and me you will have lots of sex. (I mean sex with girls, I do not have sex with Ricky. Never have done. Not even when drunk. Why would I do that? Anyway we weren't drunk, we were just high. And it wasn't sex. Just keeping warm. Why are you looking at me like that?).

Ricky

"I HAVE BEEN TERRIBLY POPULAR OVER THE YEARS."

Dirty Diana

Full name:
But you can call me … anytime.

Place & date of birth:
I was born in India, have wonderful childhood memories of being fanned by a punkawalla, can't remember his name but he had such a funny, brown face. The date I was born? Oh darling, it was a long time ago.

Occupation:
World traveller.

Favourite holiday destination & why?
I have a very modest holiday home in Torrevieja. Four bedrooms, tiny pool, no permanent staff. Although I'm thinking of making Chang, my masseur, the houseboy, since I unfortunately had to have him deported from the UK.

Favourite food?
Darling, I don't eat, it's so terribly bad for one.

Favourite type of music?
Flamenco!

Which TV shows do you watch?
I don't watch the television, darling, far too busy entertaining at home.

Do you have a role model?
Coco Chanel.

If you had to rate yourself 1–10 in attractiveness, how would you score?
Oh darling, not for me to say. I have been terribly popular over the years though. Even if I do say so myself.

What has been your greatest accomplishment in life?
A wonderful young flamenco dancer in Alicante. He moved like an animal, on the dance floor and off!

my FAVOURITE HOLIDAY

by Noreen Maltby

Hello! Well I must say I'm absolutely flabbergasted to be asked about my favourite holiday. To be honest I'm flabbergasted that anybody asks my opinion about anything. My son Geoff says I'm "the most boring woman in the world"! He doesn't mean it of course, he just says things for devilment, you know what kids are like.

The last few years I've been going to a little fishing village on the Costa Blanca for me holidays, it's called Benidorm and it's absolutely smashing but I think my favourite holiday ever has to have been many years ago, when my husband Ron was alive. Ron used to take us all over the country in our little car, I think it was a Daschund Cherry, lovely car which Ron absolutely adored. If fact, he loved the car so much that during the seventies he'd often take it for a run out for a couple of hours on a hot summer's evening, on his own. I'd always say, "You must be crackers, it's way too hot to go for a drive!" and sure enough he'd come back breathless and covered in sweat! I must say it was the most reliable car we ever had but I'd often find the odd pair of tights in the glove compartment. Ron said it was in case the fan belt went; once a boy scout always a boy scout, eh?!

So, one summer Ron suggested we took the car or "The Beast" as he would refer to it (I never liked that name, I wanted to call the car "Lady" after *Lady and The Tramp* but Ron was having none of it) to the Las Vegas of the East Coast, Bridlington. Well I was never one for flying in them days (not that we could ever afford to!) so I said, "Let's do it, Ron!" and we packed a couple of cases, made a flask of tea and some tinned tomato sandwiches and we was off. We got as far as Huddersfield when I realised we'd left the kids playing in the back garden! Ron was absolutely furious; he'd worked out the petrol money to the penny and this had sent the budget for the trip through the roof. Anyhow, we turned back, drove home, picked up our Pauline and Geoff (or Geoffrey as we called him then) and set off at double speed. It was about 120 miles from Wigan to Brid so by rights it shouldn't have taken us two days to get there but we had plenty of sandwiches (thank goodness I always make too many!) and in them days when your flask ran out you just knocked on somebody's door and asked if you could use their outside tap. Sleeping in the car wasn't my favourite part of the holiday and what with the hot nights and nowhere to change clothes, by the time we got to Paradise Caravan Park in Bridlington

> ## 'The Las Vegas of the East Coast, Bridlington.'

I looked like I'd been gang raped! Geoff and Pauline were no bother at all though, Pauline liked sleeping in the boot. She once had to do that when we came back from a Spinners concert in Harrogate. Ron met a couple of women from Wigan that he knew at the interval and offered them a lift home so we all had to budge up.

I must say, even though the weather took a turn for the worse after the first night and it rained for the rest of the week, Bridlington was "spot on" for a week away. It's fair to say that Ron had a difficult time that holiday as he was struck by lightning several times (I blamed the metal plate in his head) but me and the kids had the time of our lives. The caravan park had its own club house and there was nightly entertainment for all the family. One of the acts was Billy James & His Amazing Dancing Pig; the pig couldn't actually dance but Billy used to dance around the pig to current pop music (Brotherhood of Man, Rod Stewart, that kind of thing) and the kids thought it was absolutely terrific.

One day when the rain had eased off a little (it was more spitting to be honest) Ron suggested we had a walk up to Hornsea to look at the pottery but I thought 15 miles was too far for two eight year olds to walk so I suggested we had a hike up to Skipsea because I'd read there was an animal park with some chickens in it; if the kids liked Billy's pig they be cock-a-hoop over the chickens! On a positive note that was the very last time Ron was struck by lightning and the kids had never seen an air ambulance before so in a funny sort of way it was a win win situation. There's nothing like a near death experience to bring a family together and the kids still got to play with their dad in hospital because I bought them some fridge magnets that they stuck on his head. Happy days!

'I blamed the metal plate in his head'

SOLANA

Solana Memo

To:
Mateo Castellano
CC:
From: Janey Yorke
Date & Time: Saturday 3:27pm

You are not management and should not be using Solana memo paper. Everybody knows you have a wife, stop being an arse and ring her to tell her the bad news that there's nothing wrong with you. (Apart from the fact that you are a vain, lazy, two-faced, unreliable, greasy, haired arsehole). And as for your "imije", who do you think you are? Bono?

IMPORTANT - IMPORTANTE
Please action this Memo as soon as possible.
If you need a translation call Jose on Ext 443.

DONALD & JACQUELINE'S
Budget Holiday Guide

We all know that holidays can be hellishly expensive but over the past twenty years Jacqueline and I have become rather adept at keeping ourselves (and others!) entertained while abroad for very little or no money at all. First of all, go all inclusive; I can't stress this enough. Also be extremely vigilant when it comes to the small print. On our first all-inclusive holiday we weren't told cocktails were not part of the all-inclusive deal. The last thing we expected was a bill for drinks but on that first night when I came back from the toilet I found Jacqueline open mouthed after the barman had given her one. It's such a shame to end the evening with a nasty taste in your mouth but once bitten, twice shy and I assure you we weren't caught out like that again.

> "I FOUND JACQUELINE OPEN MOUTHED AFTER THE BARMAN HAD GIVEN HER ONE."

Another dodge is for the "all-inclusive" bar to only serve "local" spirits. Don't ask for a brand-named vodka or whisky, you'll only end up paying for it. Of course you'll end up paying for the local stuff in other ways; Jacqueline quickly realised the "local" vodka at the Solana has some curious side effects. The first time she sampled six or seven double shots of "Caliente" brand vodka she became terribly, how can I put this? Loose. Now a minor irritation like this shouldn't spoil your holiday of course – in Neptune's we just moved to a table nearer the ladies powder room and in the bedroom I simply made "other arrangements".

Do make sure your "all-inclusive" holiday also includes FREE trips. From demonstrations of vegetable juicers to watching a man fold a napkin into 100 different animals, we've been on some shocking trips in our time but the main thing was they were all FREE. Naturally you will be offered things to buy on these trips but you must stand firm. We find the best way to reply to an offer of buying a €250 juicer is to simply change the subject.

Example:

SALES REP:
So that concludes the demonstration of the Boost Blaster 2000; we hope you enjoyed the complimentary juices that were on offer today.
DONALD:
We certainly did, gracias.
SALES REP:
Would you be interested in owning a Boost Blaster Juicing Machine?

DONALD:

How wonderful, we'll have two, thank you. I must say we didn't realise the machines, like the juices, were also free.

SALES REP:

Erm, no it's not, you have to pay for it.

DONALD:

Oh good heavens no! (laugh heartily here at the very thought of it). Now, could you please point us in the direction of the free coach to take us back to the all-inclusive Solana.

SALES REP:

But it's on special offer.

DONALD:

Have you ever visited the Lochs of West Scotland? The air this time of year can be most agreeable.

SALES REP:

No, I haven't. The Boost Blaster is discounted to half price today.

DONALD:

You have beautiful eyes, is that their real colour or are they contact lenses? (Flattery is a great diversion tactic, and it also, very occasionally, can lead to other interesting "areas".)

SALES REP:

We cannot board the coach back to the Solana until I have sold at least one of these machines.

DONALD:

Best of luck, my dear, let us know when you've done that, we'll be sitting over by the remaining gratis fruit juices.

"IT'S AMAZING WHAT HARDENED SALESMEN WILL OFFER TO GET RID OF YOU ONCE YOU GET DOWN TO YOUR G-STRINGS."

So, you see how it goes. Don't give in; it's a bit like when Jehovah's Witnesses come to your house; let them knock, the paint lasts longer than the skin. Jacqueline and I often go to timeshare holiday sales weekends, these wonderful FREE breaks involve intensive "hot house" sales techniques where unsuspecting couples have been known to go home in tears after spending thousands of pounds signing up for the same random NON-INCLUSIVE holiday for two weeks a year for the rest of their natural lives. Now did you spot the vital word in that last sentence? UNSUSPECTING! Forewarned is forearmed, be prepared to sit in a room and be shown videos and slides for up to eight hours at a time. Just remember, the longer you sit there, the more money you are SAVING. Tea, coffee and often biscuits are free throughout the day. Alcohol is often provided but please remember, this can affect your judgement. Best to stick to soft drinks – a cola or lemonade costs just as much as a tea or coffee in most cafes and restaurants these days so you are saving exactly the same amount of money! Admittedly the selling techniques employed during these weekends are severe and demanding, after enduring a 12 or 13 hour sales pitch on a four-bedroom, split level finca in Torrevieja one does need a back-up plan and ours is one that has never let us down. Just at the point where you are considering taking out your VISA card and paying your £1,000 deposit, just so the sales people (yes, there will be more than one) shut up and let you out of the building for some air; simply start to touch each other in an inappropriate manner. This tried and tested technique has NEVER let us down. On the contrary, it has, on one occasion, led to us to actually making a PROFIT! It's amazing what hardened salesmen will offer to get rid of you once you get down to your g-strings.

SOLANA

DICKY DOUGHNUT'S KIDS CLUB

Come see Dicky Doughnut in his magical Doughnut world (*The Hawaiian Function Room*) with his wife Doris Doughnut and Lucifer their crazy dog.

Fun, games and prizes all day for all children under 14.

Games include:

HOW MUCH? - Guess the amount of change in Dicky's trouser pocket.

JUMPING JACKS - Do star jumps on the spot after lunch, last one to be sick gets a prize.

MUSICAL STATUES – Music is played then when it stops see how long you can stay still, as still as a statue! Prize given if the record of 3 hours 8mins is broken.

COUNT ALONG WITH LUCIFER - Count the fleas on Lucifer's coat but be careful, they jump!

Please note: while every care is taken to look after your loved one sometimes accidents do occur. Let's leave it there shall we? ...

Stylish sophisticated cabaret

Style & Glamour

WELCOME TO NEPTUNE'S ⚓ BAR ⚓

Stars of tomorrow

Neptune's is The Solana's very own stylish cabaret bar and eatery with all the luxurious and thrilling attractions of a Las Vegas showroom. Style and glamour are the watchwords here where the Benidorm elite meet to eat and rub shoulders with the stars of tomorrow.

Shaun Foster Conley

A "DRINK AS MUCH AS YOU CAN" POLICY

NEPTUNE'S WAS LAUNCHED IN the long hot summer of 1990 and was the brainchild of the then CEO of Solana Resorts, Ramón Delgado. A notorious alcoholic and sufferer of clinical schizophrenia, Ramón believed he was a Spanish pirate and built the exterior of Neptune's in the shape of a pirate ship complete with portholes, rigging and sails. Ramón had to step down from the post of Solana CEO after Neptune's opening night when he shot four holiday makers, two waiters and a DJ and killed the head barman, Edwardo Longoria, by dragging him onto the roof of the building and making him walk the plank (fall ing 40 foot head first into a skip).

Neptune's stands on the site of The Solana's previous nightclub, The Red Lion. The Red Lion was one of the more notorious English bars in Benidorm in the early eighties and was owned by infamous karaoke hostess Gina Wallace. Gina was wheelchair bound but this didn't stop her being the life and soul of the party. Her trademark number was to sing the Benny Hill classic "Ernie (The Fastest Milkman in The West)" while propelling herself in her wheelchair around the club, throwing cartons of milk at patrons which would explode on contact. Was Gina an early exponent of performance art or just a mad old bitch who enjoyed soaking customers in out of date milk? Sadly we'll never know as Gina died on a Disabled Charity fun run in 1989 dressed as a bottle of strawberry Yazoo.

THE WOMAN WHO PUT THE "COCK" IN "COCKTAILS"

NEPTUNE'S HAS A "DRINK AS MUCH as you can" policy. Most all-inclusive bars merely have a "drink as much as you want" policy but we find it's much more fun to actively encourage British national traditions and binge drinking is no exception. Can't decide what to drink?

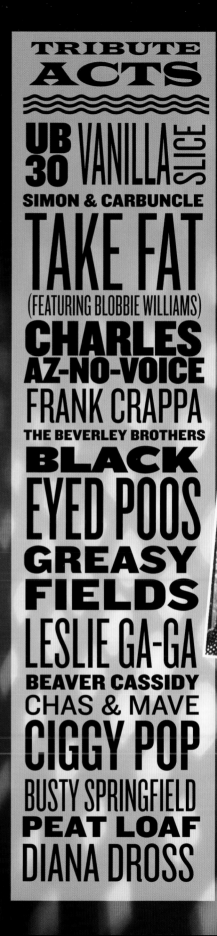

TRIBUTE ACTS

UB 30 VANILLA SLICE

SIMON & CARBUNCLE

TAKE FAT
(FEATURING BLOBBIE WILLIAMS)

CHARLES AZ-NO-VOICE

FRANK CRAPPA

THE BEVERLEY BROTHERS

BLACK EYED POOS

GREASY FIELDS

LESLIE GA-GA

BEAVER CASSIDY

CHAS & MAVE

CIGGY POP

BUSTY SPRINGFIELD

PEAT LOAF

DIANA DROSS

FOOD

Neptune's is fortunate to have the full Solana menu PLUS nightly specials. Now that the salmonella outbreak of 2001 is a decade behind us we remember the eleven holidaymakers who tragically died with a commemorative seafood menu – Oceans Eleven! Eleven brand new fishy dishes are waiting to tantalise your tastebuds; from mouth-watering mains such as Jellied Eels in a Rum Sauce to decadent desserts including Crab Crumble and Squid Soufflé. Janek our Polish chef may not have been brought up by the ocean (although he has brought up several things INTO the ocean, he gets terrible sea sickness) but he DOES have a mullet! (Do you see what we did there?!)

W h y not ask advice of the lovely Lesley (the woman who put the "cock" in "cocktails"), our resident mixologist. A mixologist is not merely someone who encourages you to mix your drinks (something we actively promote to get that party atmosphere going; unless of course you're going for the squid soufflé) but a bartender who has attained a high level of expertise in the creation of cocktails. One dictionary definition of a "cocktail" is "a mixture of substances or factors especially when dangerous or unpleasant in its effects", and on this score Lesley doesn't disappoint. In fact if you can drink five of Lesley's homemade cocktails one after the other you win a free t-shirt (although you'll probably need help putting it on).

NEPTUNE'S IS PROUD TO PRESENT THE WORLD'S MOST COMPREHENSIVE LIST OF TRIBUTE ACTS

THESE DAYS AS WELL AS SHOWCASING Benidorm favourites such as Shaun Foster Conley, Asa Elliott and zany comedy vocalist Cheroot we try and give a home to our more seasoned performers, acts who once graced the stages of Britain's most famous variety theatres and are now in the twilight of their careers.

From Dilly Shaft and her Performing Mice to Basil Kole and his infamous quick change act "Travels Around My Mother', these are the forgotten gems who have entertained heads of state and royalty since the turn of the last century. A Costa Blanca favourite is the legendary Mal Jolson. Mal started his career in the late sixties as "Moby Dick", one of Benidorm's first ever male strippers. Thankfully he now keeps his "monster of the deep" tight inside his pants as he wows his army of fans with songs ranging from "April Showers" to "California Here I Come". Mal would like to thank his loyal fans for supporting him during his recent multiple rape court case where he was found not guilty on all charges and thrilled members of the jury with an impromptu rendition of "You Made Me Love You" after the verdict was read out.

NEPTUNE'S

BAR

THE STORY CONTINUES...

Neptune's also strongly believes in promoting
the undiscovered acts of the future.

Recent bookings include Mathew & Son, Peat Loaf,
Shoewaddywaddy, Miguel Jackson, Trannie Lennox,
drag act Sheila Bilge and a Bananarama tribute act.

As we enter an age of digital entertainment
and special effects here at Neptune's we believe
the cornerstone of any good holiday is great food,
face numbing alcohol and good old fashioned entertainment.

With this in mind come and visit us during your next
holiday in the sun and we will prove to you that entertainment
is not dead, it just has severe breathing difficulties.

Hasta luego!

The staff and regulars at Benidorm's premier nightspot.

Dodgey Dick's

AIRPORT RUN

We all know the scenario, it's the last day of your holiday and you've got hammered in a bar or café, lost track of time and missed your transfer to the airport.

Worry not dear traveller, Dodgey Dick's airport run is the best available in Benidorm. Why pay through the nose for a licensed Spanish taxi when for €40 you can lie back and enjoy the luxury of Dick's vintage 1991 "Renault Panic".

A full choice of music is available for your listening pleasure, everything from Johnny Mathis to Abba (please note some 8 track cassettes are unplayable due to a mouse infestation in the early eighties).

Listen to a never ending succession of anecdotes from Dick's rich and varied life. Dick's had the good, the bad and the ugly (mainly ugly) in the back of his car including many local celebrities including that alcoholic who got sacked off *Coronation Street* and a member of Black Lace.

When booking this service on a Fri or Sat night please allow an extra 30 minutes as Dick is usually pretty pissed by 9 p.m. and will probably need a few café con leches to sober up a bit.

If booking in high season please be aware, Dick's car has no air conditioning and sadly the last of the handles to wind down the back windows snapped off in early 2005.

Safety first – If at the time of your transfer Dick is absolutely arseholed (Fiesta weekends and Manchester City games) we have the right to send out Mucky Mick, Dick's deputy. (Please note: Mick does not help with heavy luggage, chain smokes and can smell a bit ripe Aug/Sept).

The seats felt damp
Mrs Jordan, Saddleworth

A shattering experience
Simon, Aberdeen

I've never been so scared in my life
Hugh, London

Call +34 058 88733

SOLANA

NEW for the Solana in 2011

Internet Room!

Always at the cutting edge of technology The Solana Resort is proud to present its very first Internet Room.

4 top of the range computers available, 1 x Commodore 64, 2 x 128K ZX Spectrum, 1 x Atari Console.

- SEND EMAILS HOME!
- CHAT TO FRIENDS AROUND THE WORLD!
- SURF THE INTERNET!
- SEND MORE EMAILS HOME!
- CHECK ONLINE WEATHER TO SEE WHEN IT WILL STOP RAINING!
- ONLY 1 EURO PER HOUR!

We haven't quite managed to get the Atari online as yet but we can offer you a highly challenging game of 'PONG' while we wait for an engineer.

www.
solanabenidorm
.com

Mick Garvey's
HOLIDAY HUSTLES

Hola! Mick Garvey here with some essential money saving tips to double your dosh and keep your euros for yourself!

I know if you've got any sense at all you'll be on an all-inclusive holiday which means keeping tight hold of your hard earned cash and only dipping in your pockets to keep your hands warm. But there are those times when you'll be forced out of the sanctuary of your all inclusive and find yourself in restaurants and on day trips which mean you have to dish out the dough. DON'T PANIC, Uncle Mick is here to show you all the devious dodges and wonderful wangles you can get up to, all the time keeping a lid on those savings and sometimes even showing you how to go home with more moolah than you came out with … Read on!

#1 THE BIRTHDAY BAMBOOZLE

An oldie but a goodie, this scam is simplicity itself. All you need is to be able to sing, and not even in tune – save that for the karaoke later in the evening! In any restaurant, in any city, in any part of the world all you need to do to get a few freebies is to sing happy birthday. Don't worry if you don't speak the lingo of the country, the tune to Happy Birthday is the same the world over! OK, you might only get a free drink or maybe a slice of complimentary cake but it's better than a poke in the eye. And it's FREE!

#2 THE BED BUG BUNCO

Never check into your hotel without a matchbox full of bugs. Ants, fleas, cockroaches, whatever you can find. As soon as you are shown into your room call down to reception and ask for a manager to come up to the room asap (it helps if you can get your wife or daughter to scream in the background during this call). Just as they arrive and knock on the door open your matchbox and throw the contents onto the pulled-back bed sheets. The manager will come in and see the horrific sight and offer you untold riches (or at least a move to a room with a sea view) to keep your trap shut about their crappy accommodation!

#3) CELL PHONE SWINDLE

This is a great lunchtime scam if you're dining alone. Take your table and put your shopping bags on the back of the chair. First of all order a drink from the menu then, as it arrives make sure you are on your mobile phone. As your drink arrives tell your waiter what food you want (while still on the phone) then give the waiter a "thumbs up" as you leave the restaurant saying "Hang on, I can't hear you". Go outside, finish your call and come back to your meat and two veg. Scoff that then do EXACTLY the same routine when you order your pudding. Finally order a coffee, go outside while talking on your phone then when you get out of vision take to your heels and off you go. Why won't the staff be after you like a robber's dog? (Here comes the Derren Brown mind-bending shit) Because you've already been outside a couple of times and come back they won't think nothing of it. PLUS (and here's the best bit) you've left your bags on the back of your chair; you'd be crazy to leave them, right? WRONG! The designer bags you bring in are filled with bog paper you nicked the last time you were in there! Haha! Genius or what?!

#4) THE HEART ATTACK HOAX

Pretty straightforward this one: you get to the last course of your meal then you do a "dying duck", falling face first into your apple pie screaming in agony as you clutch your achey breaky heart. As the ambulance arrives nobody's gonna ask you to pay the bill as you go to meet your maker. When at the hospital you make a miraculous recovery and get back out onto the town ready for a bit of post-dinner karaoke. Again, quite a hard core one this but hey, nothing ventured nothing gained; do you want that free meal or what?!

#5) THE TERMINAL ILLNESS SCAM

OK, this is a bit more advanced and you have to have fairly flexible morals but we did this for a few years and got great results. When you are seated ask the waiter if you can see the manager, tell him your son/daughter "hasn't got long left" and that coming to his restaurant was on your kiddy's "bucket list", one of things to do before he/she dies (this could also be true!). Wipe away a tear and ask if it is OK to have a photo taken with the staff for the local newspaper. I've not had one place that gave us a bill at the end of the meal yet. Don't forget, you're not telling any lies, saying your beloved "hasn't got long left" could be referring to your holiday! And as for a bucket list, just having one doesn't necessarily mean you're gonna croak it. So go ahead with this cheeky dodge with a completely clear conscience. Unfortunately we've had to stop doing this scam as when she got to about 12 Telle started refusing to have her head shaved.

GOOD LUCK WITH YOUR HOLIDAY SCAMS AND REMEMBER, IT'S NOT THEFT, JUST REDISTRIBUTION OF WEALTH. NOBODY GOES HUNGRY WHEN THEY'RE ON HOLIDAY WITH MICK GARVEY!

"I HAVE MY FINGERS IN MANY PIES"

Mr Pink

Full name:
My name is Mr Pink. And before you ask no, it's not my name and yes I did choose it.

Place & date of birth:
Many long, dark years ago in Southend on Sea. I was born in Southend because I wanted to be close to my mother, she lived there at the time. I left school at 14, you could say I attended the University of Life then went into National Service where I was an entertainer. Female impersonation was my forte although I preferred the title "gender illusionist". That was a long time ago and I've been in Spain for the last 25 years where I have my finger in many pies.

Occupation:
Businessman/Entrepreneur.

Favourite holiday destination & why?
I don't do holidays, dear. When you run your own business, if you don't work you don't eat.

Favourite food?
Jellied eels, winkles, cockles, mussels, anything that reminds me of my youth in glorious Southend on Sea.

Favourite type of music?
I like proper music, not that rubbish they play now. These days kids think Doris Day is a bank holiday.

Which TV shows do you watch?
Television rots the mind. I prefer films, dear. Anything from the golden era. Betty Grable, Greer Garson, Ava Gardner, Bette Davis. As a boy I had posters of them all over my bedroom wall; my mother was quite surprised I didn't marry.

Do you have a role model?
Possibly Uri, my personal bodyguard. He's the strong, silent type and although officially under me, I certainly look up to him. But then at five foot two I have to look up to everyone, dear.

If you had to rate yourself 1–10 in attractiveness, how would you score?
I would say 9 but then I've always been my strongest critic. I asked this question to Uri last night when he was brushing my hair before bed. He said, "Sir, you know how I feel, you can always rely on me to give you one". Funny, I thought he'd have rated me higher than that.

What has been your greatest accomplishment in life?
There are so many. I had a Wild West Theme Park and that was going wonderfully until a rather tragic accident occurred. Thank goodness all the employees were illegal immigrants or I'd have had hell to pay. I suppose my race track gives me the most pleasure, it's both my hobby and a business. I like to settle old scores on the track and I always win. Well, I say always; there was this one time … No, I don't want to talk about it.

SPOT THE DIFFERENCE 2

Did you spot the difference?

Answer on page 152

KARAOKE
DIVORCE

Divorce parties are all the rage and of course no party is complete without karaoke.
Here are our top ten divorce favourites.

1. D.I.V.O.R.C.E. – *Tammy Wynette*
2. HE'LL HAVE TO GO – *Jim Reeves*
3. I HATE YOU SO MUCH RIGHT NOW – *Pink*
4. CRY – *Johnnie Ray*
5. YOUR CHEATING HEART – *Hank Williams*
6. HAVE I TOLD YOU LATELY THAT I (DON'T) LOVE YOU? – *Van Morrison*
7. I WILL SURVIVE – *Gloria Gaynor*
8. HEARTBREAK HOTEL – *Elvis Presley*
9. WHEN YOUR LOVER HAS GONE – *Billie Holiday*
10. BAD ROMANCE – *Lady Gaga*

Health And Safety Incident Report

Incident Date: 28th September 2007
Incident time: Aprox 3pm
Incident Location: Levante Beach
Incident Event: Wedding organised and catered for by Solana, Benidorm
Person(s) involved: Mr Mel Harvey, Mr Geoff Maltby
Injury sustained: Severe Concussion

Summary of Incident:

We had been commissioned by Solana client Mr Mel Harvey to plan and execute (probably bad choice of word that) a Hawaiian style wedding on the Levante Beach. Everything had gone to plan and local drag queen and part time vicar Jordan Rivers was conducting the ceremony. My view was slightly obscured as I was playing the "Wedding March" on the organ at the time but from what I could see a large man who was paragliding close to the shore lost height and ploughed into the wedding party, kicking Mr Harvey in the head and knocking seven bales of shite out of him (pardon my French). The paraglider turned out to be Mr Geoff Maltby (also a Solana resident although not invited to the party) who was also concussed after being dragged for another ½ mile along the sand before becoming airborne again. Both Mr Harvey and Mr Maltby were admitted to hospital under their own insurance policies. I must stress that having an uninvited guest at this Solana function at no time compromised the guest's security and Mr Castellanos (head barman) had twice ejected Mr Maltby on his previous failed attempts to join the wedding.

Signed: *Janey Mare.*

Witnessed by: *Mateo*

SOLANA

Kenneth's Caps

Fit As	Bummer	Sex God
Available	Easy	Hot
Fierce	4 Sale	Friend of Dorothy
Beguiling	BANDIT	F.A.F?

Aqua Aerobics

Aqua Aerobics today at
10am with Mateo

Pool Noodles provided
(various flavours available)

Please note, we cannot accept
any responsibility for mental anguish
caused by Mateo's water
aerobics uniform.

w.solanabenidorm.com

SOLANA

When you come to Benidorm you must buy lots of crap that has the word "Benidorm" on it for all your friends. This is the law in Benidorm. If you are caught in Alicante airport trying to leave after a holiday in Benidorm without any crap or "tat" as the English call it, you will be sent back in a taxi (at your own expense) and forced to buy twice as much as you would have bought in the first place. Here is my list of the best crap or "tat" Benidorm has to offer.

Another very popular item, it cannot exactly be called good taste but it is still not Benidorm tat. Sure it has the word Benidorm on it but there are better ways of showing your love.

Benidorm T-Shirt

Benidorm Hat

Benidorm Bat & Ball

This is the classic Benidorm gift, they are made extra large to fit fat, English heads. Although this is a popular gift it is almost borderline tat; it is actually too stylish and subtle to be true Benidorm tat. Take one of these by all means but keep buying.

A variation on the t-shirt, this is a little bit more like it, show people where your heart lies when you are freezing on the beach in Scarsborough or Blackpool. Although this could be tackier (black is a cool colour) it certainly is a good starting point before you get into the more serious Benidorm tat.

Benidorm Cosh

Flip Flop Fridge Magnet

Now this is more like it. I know what you are thinking, you are thinking, Mateo, 1) What the hell is this and 2) Why the hell would I buy it? Well, my answers are simple, 1) It is a small ceramic flip flop which is a magnet so you can place it on your refrigerator at home and 2) I have no earthly idea. But the fact is this is top Benidorm tat and you must buy it.

So here we have another magnet for your refrigerator, OK this one has a bottle opener on it so you can get drunk and sing "Sweet Caroline" in your living room pretending you are still in Benidorm but look at what it is. It is a cow in a hot air balloon, the balloon is Benidorm. IT MAKES NO SENSE! But it does not matter, it is Benidorm tat that helps you get drunk so you must buy it.

Fridge Magnet Bottle Opener

Mateo's TOP TAT

This is top lethal Benidorm tat. This is not a bat to play baseball, this is a cosh also known as a policeman's truncheon. If you hit someone over the head with this (and that is exactly what it is designed to do) you will kill them. I am lost for words. But you will buy this just to show your friends back home how crazy people in Benidorm really are.

We have plates for one reason, to eat food from them so why the hell do you need a bumpy plate which is difficult to eat from? Because you are not supposed to eat from this plate, you have to put it on a shelf and look at it to remind you when you were in Benidorm. Who cares that you have hundreds of photographs you took on holiday, you need a plate, with dolphins on it. I have never seen a dolphin in Benidorm and even if there are dolphins they cannot jump over buildings. Still, for 8 euros this is top (but expensive) Benidorm tat.

Benidorm Plate

Benidorm Thermometer

Oh my goodness, this one makes me laugh most of all. Not only are you looking at a picture of Benidorm, you have a thermometer to show you how cold you are in England! Ha ha ha! This is the people of Spain laughing in your face twice! Once that you bought something so strange and ugly but twice because you are looking at it in the cold! €6, mid-priced Benidorm tat.

Benidorm Ashtray

What can be more romantic than an ashtray? That's right, an ashtray with the word Benidorm on it. This has written on it, "I've been to Benidorm and Remembered You". Wouldn't it be quicker to just say, "I hate you"?

When you said you were going on holiday to Benidorm did anyone say, "Can you buy me a tall ceramic house that I can pour my favourite drink from"? No, of course they didn't, they said, "Get me 400 Silk Cut and a 4 litre pump dispenser bottle of vodka". But still you bring them back a weird house that has a tap on the front of it. Do houses in Benidorm look like this? Of course not. Do people in Spain pour drinks from small ceramic houses? They do not. This is bizarre, unexplainable, Benidorm tat.

With the possible exception of the flip flop refrigerator magnet, this is probably Benidorm tat in its purest form. Absolutely pointless and totally without function. Even the painting/sculpture of the beach is wrong. The Levante beach is not square, you cannot hire parasols which are 12 times bigger than a human, I could go on but you get my message, at 4 euros this is the ultimate Benidorm tat, buy it for your friends and see them stare at you with their mouth open.

Cock Nose Glasses

OK, OK, I know this does not say Benidorm on it in writing but it has Benidorm written all over it! (Can you see what I did there???). This is my all time favourite Benidorm tat, Cock Nose Glasses. Put these on your face and you will have a cock for a nose! (I can hardly write this for tears of laughter running down my face.) And look, you can buy the hat and glasses for under €6; so you can look like a cock and a c**t all at the same time!!!

Benidorm has some amazing attractions. It's not all English breakfasts and bingo and there are many excellent guide books helping you to unlock the majesty and wonder of this jewel in the Costa Blanca crown. But here are just a few gems that might pass you by.

▼ Pablo and the Dolphin

Situated just before the Levante Beach on a busy roundabout, this ancient statue of Pablo and the Dolphin is something which may escape your notice in your hurry to enjoy the sand and Mediterranean waves. A beautiful and unapologetic monument to a man who loved his dolphin; some would say from this picture, a little too much.

▲ The Cavern Club

Many people know The Beatles first embarked on their career in Hamburg, but what few fans realise is after their Teutonic triumph in 1960, they had a two day trek in a clapped out touring van from Germany through Austria, Switzerland and France until they eventually surfaced in Spain where they happened upon a small club in Benidorm called The Cavern. The rest, as they say, is history. For those who cannot travel to Benidorm to see The Cavern, a replica of the club (although sadly not as impressive as the original) has been built in the UK in Mathew St, Liverpool, L2.

◀ Ronnie & Reenie

This beautiful statue "She Wolf with Ronnie & Reenie" stands in the main piazza in Benidorm's popular theme park "Terra Mitica".

Ronnie and Rene were, legend has it, illegitimate children of one of the first English people to have a package holiday in Benidorm sometime in the early sixties.

Of course in those days Benidorm was a small fishing village and Doris Winnack, a teenager from Cleethorpes was holidaying with her parents; just a regular, ordinary, overweight 16 year old child, happy to be in the sun with not a care in the world. That was until she ran to the ladies toilets in La Rana restaurant with what she thought was explosive, chronic wind. Well, chronic wind it wasn't, twins it was! Whom Doris named Ronnie & Reenie after her mother and father who were patiently waiting for her in the restaurant but just a few feet away. But Doris couldn't go back to her parents, finish off her espresso and say, "Oh, Mam, I had twins in the bog, can you pop them in your shopper until we get back to the hotel."

No, this was the sixties and illegitimate twins would have brought much shame and embarrassment to Doris and her family.

So Doris did what any conscientious sixties teenager would do; she rolled them in toilet paper and shoved them out of the window, hoping they would somehow fend for themselves having inherited some of her plucky Yorkshire ingenuity. Well, of course, they didn't. They were newborn babies, they didn't even know they were from Yorkshire. But luckily, as legend has it, a female wolf from high in the Spanish mountains was rummaging around the back of the restaurants for scraps and took the mewling and puking babies, raising them as her own in the wilds of the Spanish "Sierra Helada".*

A crude but well meaning copy of "She Wolf with Ronnie & Reenie" stands in the Museo Nuovo in the Palazzo dei Conservatori, Rome.

*Rumour has it that Ronnie & Reenie were reintroduced into civilisation in the late eighties and are currently employed as waiting staff at the world famous Benidorm Palace.

Benidorm

▶ The Campos Bulb

In 1979, Spanish inventor and caterer Andreas Campos was struggling to see as he tried to serve his customers late into the evening in his kebab shop in the infamous "British Square" area of Benidorm. Two 40 watt light bulbs just wasn't cutting (or serving) the mustard (many were given garlic sauce or mayonnaise by mistake). So one night in his inventors shed, at the bottom on his garden in nearby Albir, Andreas invented the first ever fluorescent light bulb; now ubiquitous in kebab shops all over the world. A monument to Andreas can be found on the promenade in Benidorm in the shape of a 40 foot fluorescent bulb with the inscription: "Andreas Campo – Esperemos que tu kebab siempre contenga la salsa adecuada". (May your kebab always have the correct topping.)

SOLANA

Solana Memo

To: Janey
CC:
From: Mateo
Date & Time: Saturday 4pm

Hey, my ass has no hair, I get a back, sack + crack once a month.
And if you mean the hair on my head that is no greese, that is hair gel.
And if I am all this things you say why don't you sack me?

IMPORTANT - IMPORTANTE
Please action this Memo as soon as possible.
If you need a translation call Jose on Ext 443.

DIRECT FROM HIS SELL OUT SHOWS IN HELMAND PROVINCE

THE SOLANA GROUP ARE DUBIOUS TO PRESENT

BILLY BENIDORM

CHILDREN'S ENTERTAINER TO THE STARS

THE KIDDIES' FAVOURITE

AMAZING BALLOON SCULPTURES

WITH MAGIC HELPERS

MEET BILLY'S HELPERS, CARNEY THE COCKROACH AND MAGICAL MAZ THE FRIENDLY FAIRY. BUY THEM A DRINK AND THEY'LL SING ALL AFTERNOON!

WHAT PEOPLE SAY:

"THE SWEETS TASTED FUNNY" - DARIO CANUSO AGED 9.

"PLEASE DON'T MAKE ME GO BACK" - MICHAEL GARVEY

"I WATCHED THE SHOW AND THANKED GOD I AM IMPOTENT" - MARTIN WEEDON

EVERY SATURDAY AFTERNOON IN NEPTUNE'S

2pm until they get bored

All complaints directed to: Anthrax Entertainments, Carre Guadloa, Albir, Spain

DONALD & JACQUELINE'S

Holiday Wordsearch

JET	BOOKING	WAVE	LATE
SUNNY	WEEK	REST	WET
SAND	HIRE CAR	BEDROOM	LAGER
BIKINI	DEPOSIT	SWEAT	GATE
MEAL	SNACK	NAKED	CLOSED

K	C	O	C	Y	D	T	S	E	R	K	N	U	P	S
N	W	A	N	K	E	C	W	V	W	T	A	S	P	P
U	N	N	A	F	P	O	L	A	T	E	C	U	B	U
P	U	H	K	A	O	C	N	W	N	W	N	C	I	N
S	P	I	E	T	S	K	L	J	B	K	E	K	K	K
I	S	R	D	C	I	C	U	F	O	O	K	I	N	G
S	D	E	P	O	S	I	W	V	O	L	R	N	I	G
O	D	C	O	C	L	A	E	M	K	A	D	G	S	E
P	E	A	B	K	X	R	E	E	I	G	E	S	P	W
E	P	R	G	S	M	O	K	F	N	E	S	M	U	S
D	O	R	A	Y	C	O	C	K	G	R	O	U	N	B
T	S	G	T	T	A	E	W	S	O	L	C	I	K
I	I	I	E	I	C	O	C	K	R	O	C	K	S	N
T	T	J	E	T	T	Z	S	D	O	X	I	B	D	U
S	M	U	T	S	I	S	E	R	D	N	A	C	K	P
C	M	S	I	J	X	B	D	E	I	C	D	N	A	S

COSTA BLANCA SNOOZE

*Covering the whole of the Costa Blanca,
your friendly, relaxed snoozepaper*

BLACK OUT

Don Black and friend.

A shock decision has rocked The Costa Blanca Players, an Amateur Dramatic group made up of British ex pats who are staging an epic show entitled "Franco! – The Musical." Local musician Jose Fiddler had already composed music for the ambitious production which curiously dramatises just one day in dictator General Franco's life. The day in question is in 1953 when then Mayor of Benidorm Pedro Zaragoza transformed Benidorm from a sleepy fishing village into the booming seaside resort it is today. Zaragoza realised the only way to attract foreign tourists to Benidorm was to have the notorious bikini ban lifted and the only man who could do that was Franco himself. Zaragoza got on his vespa and drove the eight hour journey to Madrid where he had a private audience with Franco and convinced him to lift the bikini ban. A historic story and one which is in the process of being made into The Players' epic eight hour musical but with some interesting changes; president of the Costa Blanca Players, Barry Pullen told us more: "It's a great story and we are very excited about telling it but obviously we made several changes, one of which is that we've changed the beach from Benidorm to Altea. Obviously we don't want to be seen promoting Benidorm, we've all heard quite enough about that place thank you very much, this way we tell the same story but with a little more class and refinement. We couldn't believe it when we heard Oscar winning lyricist Don Black was interested in writing the lyrics for the show. His work includes some of the greatest songs ever written, Diamonds Are Forever, Born Free, Love Changes Everything. He's also a personal friend of Marti Webb so we thought there would be some good anecdotes in the tea breaks during rehearsals". But Black refused to continue when he heard about the change of location and now The Costa Blanca Players are without a lyricist. Treasurer of the amateur dramatic group Kiki Bassett is furious, "It was a real scoop getting Don involved but now we have to start looking all over again. We heard a rumour that Ralph McTell is at a loose end at the moment but who's to say we'll be guaranteed to get him?". Mr Black was not available for comment, his agent said he was holidaying with his family in Benidorm.

Blind Faith

Restaurant owner and amateur magician Rodolfo de Jesus has thrilled diners at his legendary eatery "The Denia Drive In" by staging another publicity stunt which has amused and amazed his faithful patrons. Rodolfo is well known as a P.R. genius and since the opening of his restaurant in 1979 has staged many incredible headline grabbing stunts including the much talked about night when he made restaurant critic Sebastiano Marquez disappear after a bad review in 1985 (if anyone knows of Mr Marquez's whereabouts please contact Benidorm Police on 00 902 102 112).

Wednesday night had Rodolfo's clientele spellbound again as he drove his 1980 orange Ford Capri through the streets of Denia completely blindfolded and with a bag on his head. Local mechanic and British ex pat Roger Bebbington was amazed, "I've driven home pissed as a fart many a time and that's hard enough but to be blindfolded with a bag on your head, that's just incredible". Rodolfo started his drive from the harbour and ended up outside his restaurant El Conejo Mágico without so much as a scratch on him. The two people he ran over during the feat were said to be in a stable condition in the new Hospital de Denia in La Xara.

Rodolfo de Jesus prior to being blindfolded (Right)

Look Into My Eyes!

British ex pat and amateur hypnotist Norris Quimm is doing brisk business in his adopted home town of La Nucia. Mr Quimm who sometimes goes by the stage name of Ali Cante has hit upon a lucrative sideline when he is not on stage getting volunteers to eat raw onions or run around like chickens. A few months ago a close friend of Norris mentioned that she had spent some time in Benidorm at the request of a working relative and had never quite managed to forget the "ghastly experience". Norris jokingly offered to erase his friend's memory and when she took him up on the offer there were surprising results! "I just went through the motions, put her in a semi somnambulistic state, suggested she had never been to Benidorm and expected her to wake furious with me because it didn't work. Well, I got the shock of my life when she woke up and had no recollection whatsoever of Benidorm at all, the garish sights, the offending fast food smells, the frightful people, it had all gone!" Word soon spread and Mr Quimm was inundated with requests from British residents on the Costa Blanca who had visited Benidorm either by accident or just bad planning and wanted the memory erased.

"The whole experience has been astonishing. What started as a fun hobby has turned into a very profitable business. I've given up my job as rat catcher and am now practising hypnosis full time; I'm not actually qualified but nobody really checks those sort of things in Spain, it's one of the reasons I moved here from Torbay. I'm thinking of going a step further with the service I've been offering and instead of just erasing the Benidorm memories, actually implanting new memories of a holiday the client would enjoy just like the film *Total Recall*. It's ironic really because my new German secretary, Frau Schmitz, is a dead ringer for Arnold Schwarzenegger".

Mr Quimm has enjoyed a one hundred per cent success rate in removing grubby Benidorm memories from the distressed gentlefolk of the Costa Blanca apart from a Mrs Jill Carriageway from Moraira who unfortunately had her memory wiped completely and now spends most of her days licking windows in The Javea Rest Home For the Mentally Disturbed. If you would like to visit Mr Quimm and put your regrettable past well and truly behind you, mention the *Costa Blanca Snooze* for a 10% discount.

Miss Benidorm 2011

Ms Abbotsford wears pink vest by Stella McCartney, hair by Nicky Clarke. Ms Loland wears lavender top by Primark, hair by the council.

We are thrilled to announce the the joint winners of Miss Benidorm 2011 are June Abbotsford and Alice Loland. In a hotly contested final in The Hawaiian Function Room of Benidorm's premier hotel The Solana, the audience called it a dead heat when they could not separate Ms Abbotsford and Ms Loland in the five categories of beauty, personality, talent, formal wear and swimwear. For her talent round Ms Loland drew a spontaneous standing ovation for an Alpine yodelling routine which ended in the splits and the surprise production of two live doves from her cleavage. Ms Abbotsford drew gasps from the crowd as she repeatedly ran up the wall and backflipped back onto the dancefloor, recreating the Donald O'Connor stunt from the film "Singin' In The Rain".

In their acceptance speeches Ms Loland thanked the Lord Jesus Christ and Eric Morcambe, while Ms Abbotsford paid tribute to the other contestants with an impromptu rendition of 'Fuck You' by Cee Lo Green.

Full story page 12.

Woman Accused of Living in Benidorm Sues

An English ex pat housewife living in Finestrat has sued her husband for sending out house warming invitations describing the location of their home as "5 mins from Benidorm". She had asked him to make out the party invitations as "only 40 mins from Alicante". Mrs Cathy Boyle who tried to sue her neighbour last year for suggesting she watched ITV gave an interview to the *Costa Blanca Snooze*, "I mean it's just ridiculous, what would my friends at home say if they thought I lived in Benidorm?"

Turn to page 3 where Mrs Boyle reveals more…

Turn to page 3 where Mrs Boyle reveals more…

The Sweet Smell of Villajoyosa

Residents of Villajoyosa were cheering today as they scored a double whammy! Ongoing drainage problems which had given the lesser known holiday destination a somewhat slightly unsavoury smell in recent years were finally resolved and now all residents and visitors can walk around with their heads held high and their nostrils open! Local English ex pat and restaurateur Derek Sphinx was elated: "My restaurant is in the old part of town known as the Arsenal but in recent times it just smelt more like an arse. But now the council have really got their act together and we are all enjoying the sweet smell of Villajoyosa!". The celebratory double whammy came in the form of the drainage fiasco coming to an end and Villajoyosa winning the right to be described as 35km north of Alicante and not 12km south of Benidorm.

Film Protests Continue

Protesters in Denia continue their campaign against the filming of new Hollywood blockbuster *Therapist* starring Bruce Willis. While filming in the Costa Blanca area is nothing new, Denia residents have been horrified to learn that the Hollywood movie also contains scenes shot in Benidorm. Angry resident Leonard Smeg is furious: "We shall continue our campaign to drive these people out, what if my relatives in Bury St Edmunds watch this film and assume I live near Benidorm? I live over 50km away from Benidorm, it's sheer misrepresentation." Mr Smeg's neighbour and Bridge partner Miriam Fleck agreed: "It's absolutely disgusting, I've also just realised that if you separate the first three letters of the movie title from the rest it is actually called The Rapist. These people are laughing at us, this film will be available to watch for the rest of our lives; is this really the legacy we wish to leave for our children?" Slaphead Productions who are the Spanish service company for the Hollywood film were unavailable for comment

Letters Page

This week's letters page includes an angry missive from a Mrs Sarah Fisher of Calpe who is trying to sue Google Maps for displaying Benidorm in the same map grid as Calpe. "I have been incredibly distressed by this. I do not live in Benidorm and don't see why I should be tarred with the same brush". If her legal action fails Mrs Fisher intends to set up a campaign to have the screens of computers and laptops reduced in size so her home address no longer has to share a page with the holiday resort which offends her.

Hola, my name is Mateo. Working in a bar is not easy, it is almost like working as a special agent like the FBI in America or the MFI in England. You have to check out every single person coming into the bar and decide if they are going to cause trouble or not. Sometimes it is difficult to spot an English person who is drunk because they have strange faces and sound like they are slurring their words already (these people are from "Liverpool"). Can you spot the potential troublemakers? Look at every picture, pretend you have my job and decide if they get into Neptune's or not.

OK, you may think these guys get into Neptune's because they are celebrities (the one on the right is the giant from the Harry Potter films and the one on the left came 4th in *The X Factor* or something) but no, look at their sweaty, blotchy faces, they are already too drunk. I am tired of cleaning British vomit from the plastic chairs.

YES ☐

NO ☒

At first glance these two guys look like trouble. The man dressed as a chicken is about to take all his clothes off and the bald man has evil eyebrows. Also the chicken looks a bit too friendly for my liking, they could be moofalatas but then they wouldn't be the first in Neptune's.

YES ☑

NO ☐

These three jokers wearing fancy dress look harmless enough, yes? Not all of them. Look at the little guy dressed as the poo fly. He is using his tentacle to steal other people's drinks. Yes, I know that is his own drink but he will use this trick to take other people's drinks too.

YES ☐
NO ☒

This guy is wasted. He has mistaken the glasses on the bar for the glasses he is supposed to wear for his eyes. He is not a bad looking guy and normally would be a threat to take the best girls in Neptune's but looking like this? No contest.

YES ☑
NO ☐

This is Alan. He speaks in a strange language which no one can understand. I think he is from Liverpool. He drinks fourteen pints of lager a night and is usually sick on the karaoke equipment. All of these things would usually mean he does not get into Neptune's. But Alan does get in. He is the new duty manager.

YES ☑
NO ☐

This woman comes into Neptune's all the time, just because she is ugly does not mean she is going to cause trouble. Anyway, I know her, she is from Wigan and her name is Beryl.

YES ☑
NO ☐

Mateo's Guide to

Hola. In my job as hotel barman I meet many persons from all over the English Isles. Because of this, over the years I have been able to imagine a map of England in my head and here I have for you all the places to go to and to avoid if you are too poor for a proper holiday in Spain.

Scotland

Scotland is in the north of England, even more north than Yorkshire. Because of this people here are cold. When I say cold I mean their skin is the colour of a sheep except when they stay in the sun too long then they are like lobster. Only go to your holidays in Scotland if you want to be cold but as people from Scotland are always complaining about the price of everything when they are on holiday I think Scotland is probably very cheap (there must be one reason why people live there). I don't know how you get to the Scotland, it seems to be very far away, also you have to learn Scottish, this is a horrible language with two different dialects. One sounds as though they are whining like a dog, the other sounds like they are being sick. The food in Scotland is very, very bad. They take recipes from around the world (Italian pizza, Greek kebab, German sausage) and make it Scottish. They do this by dipping it in batter and deep-frying it. I know it sounds crazy but this is how you make food Scottish. Also Scotland is a very confusing place as the women look like men and the men wear skirts. Maybe some people in the old town of Benidorm like this kind of thing but I say avoid Scotland for a holiday.

Yorkshire

Yorkshire is in a part of the English Isles called Leeds. This is just below Scotland so a holiday in Yorkshire is a little warmer but I'm afraid just as horrible. People in Yorkshire are obsessed by football. Now you may think this is normal for England but this football is different, it is called rugby. I have never seen this rugby but judging by the Yorkshire men who talk about it all the time it is played by very fat men who drink lots of beer so I imagine the game is very slow with lots of breaks to go to the bar. Like people from Scotland, Yorkshire people complain all the time about the price of stuff (even in an all

inclusive!) so I would guess, like Scotland, Yorkshire is cheap; I think I once heard Gary George, a Yorkshire comedian in Benidorm say he bought a house for £400 so maybe the answer is to buy a house at the beginning of your holiday there and sell it at the end, you never know, you might make a profit. There is one good thing about Yorkshire, they have something called Yorkshire pudding. Oh my God, I love Yorkshire pudding. But it is not a pudding, it is something you have with your main course, I always have at least four or five with a sauce they call gravy. But you do not need to go to Yorkshire for this, you can get Yorkshire pudding anywhere in Benidorm (especially in The Geordie Bar in the Rincon, tell Stuart I sent you and he will probably give you an extra Yorkshire pudding for free). I say stay away from Yorkshire. If all you want is Yorkshire pudding and alcohol you know where to come!

Holidays in the UK

Wales

Even though people from Scotland speak a different language, sometimes you can understand what they are saying. This cannot be said for the people from Wales. When they speak Wales there is no way you can understand one word so a holiday to Wales (which is on the left hand side of England) will be expensive because there is no way you can go without taking an interpreter. Even the road signs in Wales are written in the Wales language so when you get there it is a big chance you will not be able to find your way home. I'm not sure what the food is like in Wales because all the Wales people on holiday seem to do is drink. But they seem to be happy and do not cause trouble although you may need to take some ear plugs with you, not for the plane journey but because Welsh people sing. They sing when they are drunk and they sing when they are sober (I once saw a Wales man sober, it was around lunch time for about 40 minutes). You might think hearing a Wales person sing is nice because Charlotte Church is from Wales but she is how you say, the exemption, most people from Wales cannot sing and they are not sexy like Charlotte, they look like they live in caves. I think the weather in Wales is probably not very good because when it rains in Benidorm they do not complain, it is as though they are used to it. They just drink. And sing. So all in all I would not recommend a holiday in Wales. Think about it, it must be a strange place to name itself after a big, fat, ugly fish. But then again, if you see some of the Welsh women staggering out of Café B at 5 in the morning, suddenly it all begins to make sense.

Island

Island is in a part of the English Isles to the west of Wales separated by a small stretch of water called The Irish Canal (people from Island for some reason are called Irish). There seems to be two parts of Island, Northern Island where people shout a lot and kill each other and Southern Island which seems to be a safer choice for a holiday as the people there are drunk most of the time and sleep a lot. The language in Island is called Blarney, it is not that difficult to understand and you can probably get by without an interpreter (as long as you have a bullet proof vest in the north and a cattle prod to wake people up in the south). Island is where the pop group U2 are from, but don't let this put you off, they are no longer in Island, they now live in Amsterdam so they don't have to pay tax (except for Bono who lives in Calcutta). Great places to visit when in Island are Dublin, Belfast and Edinburgh. I don't recommend the food in Island because they do not use herbs and spices, just potatoes and salt but I can recommend a local drink called Guinness. Guinness is drunk in pints and is a cross between beer, milk and liquorice; the first one will taste horrible but they get better the more you drink them. If I was offered a holiday in Island I would probably go but I would remember the lesson I learn in Benidorm: when a woman from Island says to you, "Are you up for the crack?" it does not mean she wants to sleep with you. This mistake you only make once.

London

They say you can go to London to meet the queen. There certainly seems to be a lot of queens from London in Benidorm, mainly in the old town or the nudist beach. One good thing about London is there is no language barrier, most speak regular English with no accent but a few sound like Del Boy (from The Fools & The Horses)

and say "lovely jubbly" and call you "fella" or "geezer" but this is only annoying, not difficult to understand. London is the capital of Britain which is found at the bottom of the England Isles in a district known locally as Daaaahn Saaaarf. People from London never, ever complain about the prices in Benidorm so I can assume from this London is very expensive. Food in London is not good, I once had an uncle who went to London and he said he ate in a restaurant called "Wimpy". In English this word means weak, cowardly and unadventurous so I leave you to draw your own inclusions about the food in London. The one good thing about London is that there are lots of things to see. You can see the Queen, she lives in Birmingham Palace where she sits outside in her garden on a weekend on a big chair called the throne so people can look at her and wave. You can go to Carnaby Street and see The Beatles, Oxford Street where you can buy fake perfume and Harrods which is a big shop that sells statues of Lady Diana. Of all the places in the English Isles I think London is the place I would like to go to most so this is the place I would recommend to you. However if you do not have the money to go to London I say come to Benidorm, we have The Beatles too.

Blackpool

From what I can tell Blackpool is the place that singers and comedians go back to when they cannot stand living in Benidorm any longer. The word "Blackpool" does not mean the swimming pools there are too dirty to swim in (although from what I hear I still would not recommend it), the word Blackpool is an old English word from the time of Shakespeare which means "without sun". There are two things to see in Blackpool, one is a roller coaster called "The Big One", the other is the Eiffel Tower. The Eiffel Tower of course used to be in France but it was stolen in 1986; buying stolen things in Blackpool is very easy because it is so close to Liverpool. People from Blackpool in Benidorm, apart from the ones who live here who are singers and comedians, usually run joke shops or small, dirty hotels called B&Bs (I think this has something to do with STDs). I will not recommend a holiday in Blackpool, I will suggest you come to Benidorm instead where you can get everything the same except the Eiffel Tower. But who needs the Eiffel Tower when you have Terra Mitica? Oh, and we have sun, can you get sun in Blackpool? No, you can't, I tell you this already, what's wrong with you? Don't you listen?

Another day in paradise!
¡Otro día en paraíso!

We're very broadminded.
Somos muy liberales.

Good to know you!
¡Bueno conocerle!

This is the wife, Jacqueline, no reasonable offer refused!
¡Ésta es la esposa, Jacoba, ninguna oferta razonable rechazada!

What eleven people do in the privacy of their own room is entirely up to them.
Qué once personas hacen en la aislamiento de su propio sitio está enteramente hasta él.

Is it possible to get a drink, my wife is starting to gag?
Es posible conseguir una bebida,mi esposa está comenzando a amordazar.

My husband can be quite passive with the right, sensitive kind of man.
Mi marido puede ser muy pasivo con la clase correcta, sensible de hombre.

Hold that position. I'll just rinse this under a tap.
Lleve a cabo esa posición que apenas aclararé esto bajo un golpecito.

Do you do Christmas dinner? My wife loves a good stuffing.
¿Usted hace la cena de la Navidad? Mi esposa ama un buen relleno.

I think I'll have to stop for a breather, I can't see properly.
Pienso que tendré que parar para un respiradero, yo no puedo ver correctamente.

Donald &
Jacqueline

Solana Memo

To: Mateo Castellano
CC:
From: Janey Yorke
Date & Time: Saturday 4:51pm

You're sacked.

IMPORTANT - IMPORTANTE
Please action this Memo as soon as possible.
If you need a translation call Jose on Ext 443.

Question Time

with Geoff Maltby

First of all let's get one thing straight; pub quizzes whether you take part in them on holiday or at home are not for the weak hearted. Anyone who just wanders down to his local for a pint, sees there is a pub quiz on and decides to join in on a whim should be BARRED FOR LIFE. A pub quiz is only for the dedicated and the passionate. Some people might think being able to recite the opening AND closing line from each of the 29 *Carry On* films is a waste of time; but those people will NEVER win a pub quiz. NEVER. Yes, I admit this has never come up in a quiz since I researched it in 1998 but when they do I won't be the one with egg on my face. I'll be the one holding the trophy.

I remember my first ever pub quiz, it was in my local pub, the Red Lion (most common pub name in the UK, followed by Royal Oak, White Hart and then Rose and Crown), it was a Wednesday night and I was sixteen. I'd always been one for storing facts and figures (often referred to as "useless information", oh yeah? Would you describe being Lancashire Pub Quiz Champion unbeaten for 17 years as "useless"? Yeah, I thought not) but something told me I could do better than school quizzes, something told me I should go regional. Years later I would, of course, go national and then European but let's not run before we can walk. So I'm sixteen years old, the pub was fairly busy, patrons beginning to club together into teams of four and six. I ordered a warm, frothy pint of Theakston's Old Peculier and took my seat. The landlord came over to me: "You're Noreen's lad aren't you? I know you look in your mid thirties but you're in my Gary's year at school, you can't be more than sixteen, you shouldn't have been served, son, you're too young". My reply was quick and succinct: "A young person aged sixteen or seventeen can drink wine, beer,

cider or perry (but not spirits) with a meal in a hotel, restaurant or part of a pub set out for eating meals". As I said this the barmaid came over and placed my mixed grill starter in front of me. BOOM! Take that, landlord. The quiz was about to start and as I took out my gold pen from its presentation

> WOULD YOU DESCRIBE BEING LANCASHIRE PUB QUIZ CHAMPION UNBEATEN FOR 17 YEARS AS "USELESS"? YEAH, I THOUGHT NOT...

case (later I would use a pen given to me by the great man himself, William G Stewart in commemoration of my 10,000th quiz question written for his legendary TV show *Fifteen to One*, but more of that later), a couple of fat heads came up to ask if I wanted to team up with them but I just waved them away. (Fat heads are what I call idiots who

have no place in pub quizzes, their heads are full of fat, not lean muscle, as mine is.) I still remember the opening question, "Name all six members of Monty Python". Oh God, it sounds arrogant now but I laughed, I laughed out loud, long and hard – this was going to be a piece of piss. I suppose I should mention now that comedy is kind of my specialized subject. Although to be fair it's kind of misleading to call it my specialized subject, you can't specialize when you know everything about everything. But yes, it's a subject that seems to be a recurring theme in my life; I do a lot of comedy myself but it goes over the heads of your regular Joe Schmo, it's quite mad shit that is so funny most people don't get it. My mate Barry is a mobile DJ and as he's on the road a lot of the time I don't get to see him much. I send him my jokes via text message but he never replies, my mam says that he's just ignoring me but think about it, how can you breathe, let alone text when you are convulsed with laughter? I also send them to an ex of mine in Brazil via email, she just replies with question marks "?????" but to be quite honest if she didn't do that I'd be worried, who wants to write middle

of the road shit that everyone "gets"? Anyway, the quiz started easy and just got easier, to be honest I was quite bored but my main course of shepherd's pie (not technically a shepherd's pie as it contained beef, not lamb, as I was quick to point out to the barmaid) and pudding duo of apple crumble and ice cream plus sticky toffee pudding & custard kept my interest as the scores were totted up and I was awarded first prize (a leg of frozen lamb, quite ironic really as that's what was missing from the shepherd's pie). There was a slight altercation about one question …

Quizmaster: *A table has sixty cups on it. One of the cups falls off the table, how many remain?*

I will NOT go down this road, in fact it's not even a road, it's a cul-de-sac and questions like this should be BANNED (see rules below). So what is the answer? Many people would, of course, answer 59. This is not correct but then there is no correct answer but I decided to humour these amateurs. I gave my answer as "one". Look at the question again, "one of the cups falls off the table, how many remain?". How

many WHAT??? You think they mean CUPS but obviously they mean how many TABLES. There is ONE table. On reading out the questions again during the marking the quizmaster had a slightly different intonation: "A table has six TEA cups on it. One of the cups falls off the table, how many remain?" Six TEA CUPS, not SIXTY cups. Well, needless to say I kicked off big style. "Nobody, NOBODY beats The Oracle, you wanna pose riddles? You wanna tell jokes? Audition for *Britain's Got Talent* you worthless piece of shit; don't fuck with me and don't fuck with the questions …" Sorry, sorry, I lost my train of thought a bit then. Obviously I didn't swear, I was only sixteen at the time but you get my gist? Curve balls like this will be thrown at you during your quiz career, treat them with the contempt they deserve, others might be embarrassed to hear "Maltby's lost it again, somebody fetch his mam" but for me this is merely an indication that I am standing my ground, winning is everything, losing is not in my vocabulary (Unless the question is: What was the first single released from REM's 1991 album *Out Of Time*? Answer: *Losing My Religion.)*

A word of warning, winning can be addictive (I know that's four words but you know what I mean). Some people are addicted to alcohol, some drugs, some get a kick from champagne, oh yeah, I've said alcohol haven't I? Well, anyway, my "drug" of choice is WINNING and I just can't get enough of it. At the time of writing I hold five regional and national titles including winner of the Ormskirk Meat Plate Pie Eating Competition (without the need of hospitalisation), Lancashire Indoor Hang Gliding Champion, North of England Jelly Throwing Champion (six years undefeated) and UK Under 12's Sit ups Champion – 14 stone and over category (this has been disputed as I am now over the age of sixteen but my record of 11 sit ups in one minute remains unbeaten and I am STILL the champion, I hope you are reading this Nicholas "Fat Boy" Forkin).

I suppose the pinnacle of my career would be my three years under Bill Stewart, who you probably know better as William G Stewart, quizmaster of CH4 television quiz show *Fifteen to One*. I simply refer to him as The Guv'nor. Sometimes two people just fit together,

Morecambe and Wise, Ant and Dec, Bill Haley and his Comets; it was a bit like this with me and the Guv'nor. Our mutual love of facts, figures and so called "trivia" (after reading this far you really think being a champion is trivial??) brought us together, there was nothing we could do to stop the attraction, fate played its hand and we were drawn together for three, wonderful, glorious, loving years. We didn't bum each other or anything like that; I just made up the questions for his TV show, but even though he rarely spoke to me he would give me a glance as I sat in the front row every time a contestant got one of my questions wrong; a glance that said, "You did it again, Geoff, you nailed the bastard".

My TV career is long gone and although I get weekly calls from BBC's *Eggheads* begging me to replace C.J. de Mooi, I'm afraid public recognition never sat easy with me. I was once recognised for being on the front row of the audience of *Fifteen to One* (well, I was there every programme for three years) while shopping in the Trafford Centre, Manchester and I can tell you, it wasn't nice. First "Oh, aren't you that guy off the telly?", next autographs, then public appearances, my own show; no, I'm afraid that's not for me. My private life is my private life, this I will not compromise. My respect goes out to the likes of Piers Morgan; yes, you might think he's an absolute cock but you try

living your life with people asking to take your picture when you're trying to get to the bakery section of Morrisons when they've just announced they've reduced the bread; I'd tell people to frigg off too.

So go to your pub quizzes, enjoy the beer, the food, the ambience but always, ALWAYS respect the questions. Here's a few Pub Quiz rules that may help you along your journey in the world of questions and answers. And remember, he who says "it's only a game" has never been a champion.

Geoff Maltby's Mega Pub Quiz Rules

#1 The quizmaster's decision is not final. If you know you are right you must defend yourself to the death. Not your actual death of course, that would be pointless, who's gonna hold up the trophy when they discover you were right all along?

#2 Rule 1 does not apply if the quizmaster is Geoff Maltby.

#3 All defaced papers are null and void. A good quiz competitor arrives fully equipped with doodle pad and a variety of pens.

#4 Own pens and cheat fenders can be used. Although there is no such thing as a lucky pen (luck has no place in a quiz) competitors often feel more comfortable with their own quiz paraphernalia.

#5 Internet accessible devices such as so called "Smart" phones are not to be used during the quiz. The internet is your best friend before a quiz but your sworn enemy during. Such devices should be permitted in the building as the internet is invaluable in backing up your argument when you need to prove a quizmaster wrong.

#6 So called "trick" questions are permitted (there is actually no such thing as a trick question, Q: How many UK hit singles has Tina Turna had? A: None. This is not a trick question, there is a definite answer) but riddles are NOT permitted, see essay above.

#7 Cheat fenders (a device to cover your already answered questions to deter cheating) are to be allowed at all times and at all levels of competition. These can be anything from a sheet of paper to a shoe box lid. Great for sponsorship too, I had Ginsters and Gaviscon in a bidding war in the late nineties to have their logo on my cheat fender – happy days.

#8 For every hour of play there must be at least four breaks for drinks to be replenished. You'll often find that many pub quizzes will have a break between every round. This can also be tiresome; for a champion like me it's just drawing out the inevitable.

#9 Table mascots are to be discouraged. If you need a fluffy effigy of your favourite cartoon character on the table to help you form your answers you're in the wrong building. It's not a pub you need, it's a mental asylum.

#10 Never, EVER become part of a pub quiz team. You will be sucked into petty debate, be pressured to pool your hard earned knowledge and God forbid, be forced into buying rounds.

THE MANY VESTS OF KENNETH DU BEKE

SEX & DRUGS & SAUSAGE ROLLS

YOUR FACE OR MINE?

256 BONES IN THE HUMAN BODY
BUT I COULD ALWAYS DO WITH ANOTHER

BEAUTY IS ONLY A LIGHT SWITCH AWAY

THIS VEST WOULD LOOK GREAT ON YOUR FLOOR

OPEN ALL HOURS

ASTRONAUT IN TRAINING
(WOULD LIKE TO EXPLORE URANUS)

FANCY A LICK OF MY LOLLY?

ALL DELIVERIES AT THE REAR

Lesley's Top Tranny Tips

Welcome to my very own page of top tranny tips. Here you will find an absolute treasure trove of hints and tits, sorry tips (it's these new gel nails – hellish for typing) on how to become a beautiful, convincing woman; even if just for one night!

Ever heard the story of the ugly duckling that turned into a beautiful swan? Well, this is just like that, apart from the electrolysis and gaffer tape. I've always wanted to be beautiful and could never quite achieve that in my day to day male persona of Les. Les was plain, Les was dowdy, Les was bland. But then, then I discovered Lesley and my life was filled with colour and sparkle! Yes, I was a bald, 14 stone, five foot six Geordie but with a short skirt, a dab of lippy out of Superdrug and a court shoe in a $11\frac{1}{2}$ I was transformed into a goddess, even if I say so myself. I remember the looks on people's faces the first day I walked into the Metro Centre in Newcastle wearing a knitted two piece and a pair of slingbacks – took their

breath away. I'm convinced I heard the words "mythical creature" being bandied about!

TOP TRANNY TIP #1
PAINT THAT FACE!

Somebody once said "less is more", now pardon my French but that is absolute bollocks (and that's not a word we trannies like to use too often). My advice when it comes to make up is slap as much on as possible and when you've done that, slap on a bit more. Even though I have a naturally flawless complexion I use quite a heavy foundation. If I'm out on the pull and I get lucky the last thing I want to do is wake up with a five o'clock shadow – it can be quite a passion killer just before breakfast.

TOP TRANNY TIP #2
BE HONEST

If I had a euro for every time I've been chatted up by a fella who didn't know I've probably got bigger tackle than him I'd be a very rich woman indeed. Lay your cards on the table (although not your cock, bit early for that) from the beginning, it may come as a shock to your prospective other half that you are "More Than A Woman" but in the long run it'll be better for all concerned. Yes, you want screams coming from your bridal suite on your wedding night but believe me, it's much better that those screams are ones of pleasure, not of abject horror.

TOP TRANNY TIP #3
THINK LIKE A WOMAN

No matter how convincing you LOOK as a woman, you also need to THINK like a woman. You may feel glamorous in your denim ra-ra skirt and white stilettos but we can always do with a little feminine mystique (as opposed to my friend Rita Maudsley who is more feminine mistake). Here are a few subtleties which will transform you from a drag queen to a gender illusionist … When going to the lavatory always say, "I'm just goin' to powder me nose, like". Announcing you are "off for a slash" can often sabotage an otherwise perfect evening. If you have opted for a slightly cheaper, nylon wig chances are it will begin to irritate as your date progresses. Always excuse yourself and sort yourself out in private; whipping off your crowning glory while saying, "Sorry about this but I'm sweating like pig on a spit," can often bring the evening to a premature close. Take care to suppress your natural masculine interests, looking over your date's shoulder during dinner to watch the football while he's complimenting you on your appearance can sometimes give the game away. And finally mind your p's and q's while eating your meal; burping, eating with your mouth open and getting hammered are all signs that the lady may not be all she seems. And on the subject of alcohol, you might think that a white wine is very ladylike but strangely enough, a pint can actually make your hands look a lot smaller.

TOP TRANNY TIP #4
GET THE LOOK

It helps to have a good idea of someone you want to model yourself on. I personally took my inspiration from three great beauties –

Nana Miouscouri, Marti Caine and Kate Moss. But whoever it is that inspires you, make sure you choose carefully. My good friend Rita Maudsley, who I briefly mentioned before, models herself on Kylie Minogue, not the natural choice for a six foot five, 18 stone tranny with size 14 feet. I feel bad for saying this but if you're reading this, Rita, it's time to change your look. Your blind dates are singing "I Can't Get You Out of My Head" for all the wrong reasons.

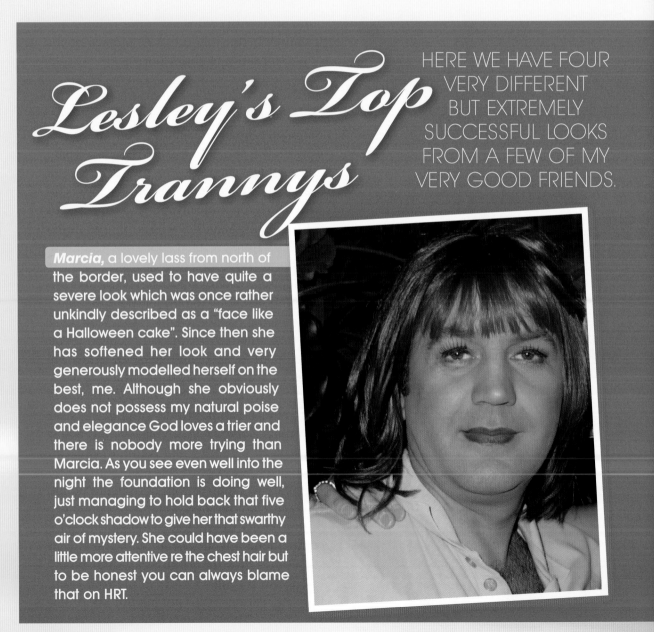

Lesley's Top Trannys

HERE WE HAVE FOUR VERY DIFFERENT BUT EXTREMELY SUCCESSFUL LOOKS FROM A FEW OF MY VERY GOOD FRIENDS.

Marcia, a lovely lass from north of the border, used to have quite a severe look which was once rather unkindly described as a "face like a Halloween cake". Since then she has softened her look and very generously modelled herself on the best, me. Although she obviously does not possess my natural poise and elegance God loves a trier and there is nobody more trying than Marcia. As you see even well into the night the foundation is doing well, just managing to hold back that five o'clock shadow to give her that swarthy air of mystery. She could have been a little more attentive re the chest hair but to be honest you can always blame that on HRT.

This is my old pal *Jordan Rivers.* She hosts a lovely show at The Ritch Bitch Cabaret bar in Benidorm Old Town. I'm not sure if you can see but she has a slight case of "one eye looking at you and one eye looking for you". Apparently some childhood injury which resulted in a magnet being lodged up her nose. But I'm sure you'll agree it does not detract from her considerable feminine charm. I said I would give her latest show, "Feminine Mystique" a plug but sadly those Spanish printers can be unpredictable and the posters came back saying "Feminine Mistake". I said go ahead, nobody would know the difference in Benidorm but she's a perfectionist that one. Anyway, go along to The Ritch Bitch down Calle Del Pal and tell them Lesley sent you, she might shove something extra in your first drink for free. (Actually I used to know an act who did that, he was called Moby Dick; "The Big Swinger" but that's another article altogether …

Now here's my old pal from London, *Titti La Camp.* Amazing that with a name like that he should grow up to be a tranny, what were the odds of that happening?! Titti, like me is all for old school glamour. Although I'm not quite sure about this pose, between you and me she looks like she's sat on the pot about to get one go but that's probably that "London chic" she keeps banging on about. More like London Shit if you ask me. Titti is currently on disability benefit as she has three asylum seekers living in her hair and is waiting on the council to serve them an eviction notice.

This is *Tiffaney,* another wonderful old girlfriend of mine from that there London. A sexy yet refined look, alluring yet noble. She can often be seen singing in various cabaret bars in the capital and as a result she needs to get changed and do her make up in very cramped and badly lit conditions. As you can see from the pic she's also a dab hand at getting ready in the dark; she tends to just throw her make up in the air and takes a running jump at it, an old trick she learnt from Cherie Blair. She does a wonderful and extremely popular medley of wartime songs including a very risque version of "Kiss Me Goodnight Sergeant Major" which has had her arrested in 5 different London boroughs. Tiff models herself on two of the greats, Ethel Merman and Bernie Winters.

KARAOKE

Have a few "close personal friends" coming over? Before you have a few drinks and relax, why not sing a few songs to ... get you in the mood.

1. COME AS YOU ARE – *Beverley Knight*
2. DO THAT TO ME ONE MORE TIME – *Captain And Tennille*
3. ALL NIGHT LONG – *Lionel Richie*
4. HOW DEEP IS YOUR LOVE? – *Bee Gees*
5. INSIDE OF ME – *Madonna*
6. BLOW GABRIEL BLOW – *Ethel Merman*
7. SOON COME – *Bob Marley*
8. LOVE HURTS – *Paul Young*
9. MR KISS KISS BANG BANG – *Dionne Warwick*
10. BUMMING AROUND – *Dean Martin*

On the tray: CORONA EXTRA LA CERVEZA

MSG Property*

(Marcus Snelling Group Property)

Are you looking for an affordable home on the Costas?
Have fairly flexible morals? Look no further!

Call Marcus Snelling today and arrange a viewing of a currently occupied home which can be yours for WELL UNDER market value.

PREVIOUS STAR PROPERTIES:

2 Bedroom apartment, shared pool, Albir. Market value: €220,000 Snelling Smashdown price: €160,500

4 Bedroom, 4 bathroom Villa, Altea Hills, private pool, Market Value: €650,000 Snelling Smashdown price: €300,000

8 Bedroom, 5 bathroom villa, private pool, tennis court, indoor bowling alley, cinema room and 3 acres of land. Market Value: €1,400,000 Snelling Smashdown price: €900,000

All properties are owner occupied. All guaranteed to be totally clueless and bewildered pensioners with no surviving relatives, no real understanding of Spanish property law, all over 70 years of age with one foot in the grave and the other on a banana skin.

Contact Marcus Snelling today. Remember there's only a few thousand euros deposit and your conscience between you and a beautiful home in the Spanish sun.

*previously 'Dead Cert Homes', previously 'Snelling Real Estate', previously 'Snelling Homes', previously 'Costly Blanca Estates'

1GP 1GP

Ooh La La, it's...

LESLEY GA GA!

From the people who brought you Lesley's Country & Western Roadshow, a brand new act for 2011 - Lesley Ga Ga, the ULTIMATE Lady Ga Ga tribute act!

Lesley and her resident house band 'The Monsterettes' bring you all of the EXCITEMENT, all of the GLAMOUR and all of the **HITS of Lady Gaga!**

BORN THIS WAY

ALEJANDRO

TELEPHONE

PAPARAZZI

JUST DANCE

POKEY FACE

JUDAS

And unlike Lady Ga Ga, this one really does have a cock!

Don't delay, pick up your TELEPHONE and book the one and only

LESLEY GA GA!

Call Lesley now on Benidorm +34 0887 6765

Classified Ads

Items for sale

Reinforced sun lounger. Would suit VERY generously built man or obese woman. As seen on *The Jeremy Kyle Show.* €30. PO Box 873.

Penguin for Sale. Exactly the kind they have at Terra Natura. But not actually one of those. I didn't steal it. Just found it. (Will not eat fish fingers, have tried). €50 ono. PO Box 887.

Father Christmas costume for sale. Some rotting from sweat stains around the groin area. €25. PO Box 932.

Lavatory paper for sale by the sheet, only used one side. Contact The Benidorm Joke Shop.

Autographs, signed memorabilia, tv stars, politicians, sports stars. Any item requested. Authentic signed colour 10x8s of William Shakespeare. Contact Snelling Memorabilia, Moraira. PO Box 431.

National Television Award, looks like a big, silver, curly butt plug. Recent unemployment forces sale. €100 ono. derrenweb@gmail.com

Hens teeth. Would suit toothless hen. €5 each. Maurice, PO Box 484.

Towels for sale. Solana logo. Can get as many as you want but only in Benidorm for 1 week. €2 each. Garvey. PO Box 364.

Various items for sale. Candles, bunches of flowers, streamers, eggs, razor blades, scarves. All could do with a good rinse. Vicky Leyton, Benidorm. PO Box 513.

All films on DVD. All good quality. Sound a bit dodgy due to popcorn being eaten in close proximity. Send for list. Snelling. PO Box 431.

Bus pass for sale. Free travel on all buses. Would suit a pensioner who looks like me. Noreen. PO Box 339.

Gas BBQ for sale. Doesn't heat up very well but besides that OK. €40 ono. Can't deliver for at least a week, currently in hospital with food poisoning. José. PO Box 245.

Items wanted

Chopsticks. Must be authentic and be able to endure heavy "all you can eat" buffet sessions. Barry, Benidorm. PO Box 106.

Drinking hat. Must be able to accommodate four full-size cans of Continental lager. Refrigerated version considered although brain freeze runs in the family. Maltby, Benidorm. PO Box 491.

House Clearances undertaken. Nothing turned down. Fast service, can call round within the hour. Especially fast service to pensioners who are not feeling well. Covers all Costa Blanca. Snelling Clearances. PO Box 431.

1950s and 1960s physique/ muscle mags. Top prices paid. Mr Pink, Benidorm. PO Box 921.

Ladies shoes, any style, size 8. Broad fittings preferred. Lesley, Benidorm. PO Box 365.

Employment wanted

Experienced dog walker. Areas covered Benidorm, Albir, Altea. All dogs must be shaved and an 8ft lead provided due to allergy to dogs. Altea Hills area. Consuela. PO Box 747.

Experienced pool cleaner. All areas covered. (This is a free ad, apologies to Mr Benitez for last week's misprinted ad "Experienced poo cleaner" – Ed) Paco Benitez. PO Box 998.

Very low cost Shiatsu massage. Just lie down and let me give you a good poke. Lesley, Benidorm. PO Box 881.

I gave Spanish lessons to England. Excrement qualifications. Pleased to see all personal certified. Only €10 pur hour. Mateo, Benidorm. PO Box 119.

Lady Garden Maintenance. Bushes trimmed. Excess foliage removed front and rear. Extra attention given to mature gardens. "Berry Khot Landscaping." Contact Mateo, Benidorm. PO Box 119.

Employment offered

Junior stylist required for Benidorm-based mobile hairdresser. Needs to be willing to work long hours for little pay. Knowledge of moped maintenance preferred. Preference given to hot Spanish guys under 30 with very little English. Email KennethduBeke@hotmail.com

Live-in Cleaner/Maid wanted for large villa. Must be able to speak English and enjoy Jacuzzi breaks with broad-minded friends. Cilla, Altea Hills. PO Box 381.

Bar staff always wanted, must have good English and strong stomach for all inclusive food. Ability to call bingo and take water aerobics classes a bonus. Apply in person at Solana Resort, Benidorm, ask for Janey.

Debt collector wanted. Immediate start. Must look threatening. Also wanted, Kung Fu partner, must be black belt 3rd dan. Scary Mary, Benidorm Caravan Park.

New skipper required for ferry to Peacock Island. Previous skipper completely off his tits on hallucinogenic drugs. Long hours, low pay. Costas, Benidorm. PO Box 193.

Classified Ads

Costa dating

Overweight, bald, unemployed man in his late 50s wltm attractive woman under 40 with own boat. Please send picture of boat. Jim, Denia. PO Box 239.

Nervous, 41-yr-old inexperienced gay seeks another gay. Age/colour/creed/sex unimportant. Must be gay though. Or at least a bit poofy. Hugh, Albir. PO Box 612.

Attractive, full-bodied, sophisticated "lady" in seek of anybody of the male gender. Absolutely nobody refused. Wheelchair users welcome. Bed bound, agoraphobic, unemployed, psychotic. I am in good health and approaching my mid forties (just don't ask from which direction). Lesley. PO Box 781.

Two guys in late 30s (very late) require 3rd broadminded guy for trips to nudist beaches. Low IQ and big feet a bonus. Derek & Mark, Torrevieja. PO Box 666.

Shy guy, strawberry blonde, gentle personality, hopelessly romantic. Seeks mythical creature. "Rough winds do shake the darling buds of May, And summer's lease hath all too short a date." Liam, Benidorm. PO Box 655.

Well preserved lady in the latter stages of life. Loves country walks, flower arranging, brass rubbing and country dancing. WLTM retired gentleman for jigsaw fun and possible anal intrusion. PO Box 315.

Hugely overweight man, slight body odor problem, sufferer of fungal infections, dandruff, hemorrhoids and chronic halitosis seeks fit woman who can cook. Absolutely no mingers. Boris. PO Box 544.

Spanish maid, works in Altea Hills, seeks television celebrities (male and female) for adult fun including sexy, hot tub action. Consuela. PO Box 883.

Gay male, 33, Michael Jackson impersonator WLTM very short, hairy, gay man to be part of my life and part of my act. Must look good in dungarees, be able to hold a mug with your feet and answer to the name of Bubbles. Micky J, Benidorm. PO Box 100.

40-yr-old single white female, needs to have a baby before everything seizes up. You: over 18, under 80, two arms, 2 legs, 2 eyes (preferably on different sides of face) and willing to have sex on first date. Jacinta. PO Box 267.

Man with convex stomach requires lady friend with concave back for mutual spooning sessions. Raymond, Rincon, Benidorm. PO Box 111.

Do you enjoy stamp collecting? Staying at home and watching television documentaries? Do you avoid parties and social functions, preferring to read a book or play Scrabble on your own? Don't write to me, you sound a right boring prick. Brandy, Alfaz del Pi. PO Box 756.

Hi my name is Julie, I'm 28, I work in HR for a large Spanish Real Estate company in Murcia. Would like to meet a handsome, single guy with GSOH. Failing that wouldn't mind trying out a bit of lezzer action. Only attractive women though: none of those women with short back and sides, practical glasses and short sleeved shirts called Pat or Roz. Lydia. PO Box 100.

Family oriented lezzer, late twenties, would like to meet gay man for mutually beneficial relationship. Must have own turkey baster. Brenda, Benidorm. PO Box 456.

Public notices

Due to overwhelming demand Benidorm Alcoholics Anonymous will now be moving to larger premises. From beginning of November we will be meeting in Cafe Benidorm, in the English Square, Benidorm. 2 for 1 on all house spirits after 9pm. As reported last week in the Costa Blanca News, €1,000 wrapped in an elastic band was dropped in the English Square area of Benidorm's new town at the weekend. Please contact us immediately as we have found the elastic band. Pam. PO Box 174.

Congratulations to Levante Beach, voted cleanest beach in Benidorm for the 22nd year running (apart from the years when it came second to The Poniente). To celebrate, free sangria all day on September 32nd, 8pm onwards.

There will be a public sales of goods in the town square, Callossa, at the end of this month. These many and varied items are all either repossessed/unclaimed. Star item: 25ft motorized bike with advertising front and rear. Would suit desperate mobility shop. Deputy Mayor, Callossa. PO Box 747.

Tuition

Symphony orchestra player offers full music tuition. No need for an instrument, I can supply. (STOP PRESS: Due to recent house burglary can currently only teach Bog Paper & Comb and The Spoons. Advice given on clicking of fingers and hand clapping too.) Leonard. PO Box 844.

Air guitar lessons offered. Novices welcome, air guitar can be supplied for a fee if you don't have your own. Ask for Big Jon at the Rock Star Bar, Benidorm.

Can't seem to get your computer to work? Have you tried turning it off and then on again? If this works please send €35 as repair charge to Marcus Snelling. PO Box 2184.

Spanish lessons for the over 50s. Preferably big women over 50. Big with large busts. Big, huge women over 50 with massive boobs. Mmmmm, big knockers.... Horace. PO Box 551.

Troy's

ESSENTIAL HOLIDAY READS

The History of Hot Pants
I love a pair of hot pants and this is the definitive history from Pan's People to Kylie Minogue.

The Wit and Wisdom of Rav Wilding by Rav Wilding
Not so much a book, more a pamphlet; he is nice to look at though.

I'll Have Fries With That by Oprah Winfrey
I often think, "I wish I could put on weight" then I read this book and I think again.

Alcohol in Moderation by Carol McGiffin
I always admire a girl who can stop at one drink and so can Ms McGiffin; as long as it's a yard of vodka.

Fitty or Fatty?
There's a fine line between a hot, chunky man (something I've been known to go for) and a Mr Blobby. With pics from Alec Baldwin to Eamonn Holmes.

Cash In The Attic by Sandy Johnson
One man's desperate tale of hiding his obsession with Johnny Cash and Country music in the loft of his Suffolk holiday home.

Living With Man Boobs by Piers Morgan
(Foreword by Rio Ferdinand)
Just when you thought a man's story of being a massive tit couldn't get any more tragic.

The Only Way is Wessex by Prince Edward
Party animal Edward spills the gossip on his crazy life.

A Hundred Years of Hair Disasters
From William The Conqueror to Boris Johnson there's been some seriously shit haircuts throughout the ages. At last here they are in handy paperback form!

Thick & Thin – The Unofficial Biography of Posh & Becks
I probably won't read this but I imagine half of the pictures will get a good fingering.

"WHEN I WAS BORN
I CAME OUT OF THE WOMAN
IN THE OPPOSITE BED"

Marcus

Full name:
Depends who wants to know. Let's use Marcus Snelling, unless it's for tax purposes then I don't have one.

Place & date of birth:
Here and there, I've always been a ducker and a diver. When I was born I came out of the woman in the opposite bed.

Occupation:
Opportunist.

Favourite holiday destination & why?
I've had some wonderful scams, er, I mean holidays in the past few years; I always try to mix business with pleasure so wherever I go be it Benidorm or Barbados there's always a deal to be done.

Favourite food?
Lunch is for wimps. I'll occasionally have a steak dinner with my glass of cognac of an evening.

Favourite type of music?
The sound of cash registers ringing. That's music to my ears.

Which TV shows do you watch?
The first five minutes of *Rogue Traders*, to make sure I'm not on it.

Do you have a role model?
Arthur Daley.

**If you had to rate yourself 1–10 in attractiveness,
how would you score?**
10. But don't ask me, take a straw poll of my girlfriends, I'm sure they'll all agree.

What has been your greatest accomplishment in life?
The bulk buying of FIFA football tickets, I can get you any seat for any game, a quick phone call to my mate Sepp and the job's a good 'un.

by *Janice Garvey*

THE BENIDORM GUIDE TO AIR TRAVEL

THE TRUTH IS YOU DON'T FEEL LIKE YOU'VE HAD A HOLIDAY UNLESS YOU'VE BEEN ON A PLANE

Yes, a walking holiday in North Wales is an option but so is that pebbledashed bread that tastes like cardboard; leave that to the miserable hippies who don't use shampoo because it's "harmful to the environment" and won't let their kids drink Sunny Delight. I'll tell you what is harmful to the environment, stinky bleeders that don't wash their pits and can't get a comb through their hair – I'm glad you won't be sitting next to me on a plane. Enjoy your weekend walking up a mountain in the pissing rain, I'm off for a week in the sun!

Cheapest Flights

Make sure you get the cheapest flights by booking mid week flights and of course avoid school holidays like the plague. Don't forget, your trip to the sun is an essential part of your child's development. If you get any hassle from annoying teachers tell them you taught your child to swim on holiday; let's see them argue that one in court. If your child can't swim just say your trip to Benidorm was educational. Every time we go there we always come home thinking, "Well, that's taught us a lesson".

Carry On Luggage

This doesn't mean a case that looks like it would belong to Sid James or Barbara Windsor, "carry on luggage" is the one you take inside the plane with you, also called hand luggage. If you're on a budget airline (and why would you be on any other?) sometimes your case can be as heavy as you like as long as it's a certain size. BUT, more and more airlines are giving this case a weight restriction.

GET PAST THE SNOTTY WOMAN AT CHECK-IN

This is ridiculous because while you're not allowed to have a bag weighing more than 5kg (about 10 lb), the man sitting next to you is probably about 4 stone heavier than you! But don't worry, I have the answer: wear a BIG coat with LOTS of pockets. Yes, if you're travelling on a hot day you might be sweating buckets but if you fill out your pockets with all the extra stuff you need you only have to get past the snotty woman at the check-in desk then it's off to Burger King to unload all your swag into your hand luggage and then you can "carry on at your convenience!"

Priority Boarding

Don't bother with all this priority boarding rubbish. Basically if your plane is far away from the gate all priority boarding does is get you first dibs on your position standing in the coach which takes you to the plane. So, first on the coach, last on the plane. Two words: RIP OFF!

RIP OFF

Delays

Make sure you bring something good to read, partly for the flight but also for delays. A two hour delay can really get your head spinning if you've got a teenage daughter with a one-year-old child and a nine year old son with ADHD. Thankfully my son's a bit older now and my daughter Chantelle doesn't come on holiday any more but it's still nicer to get lost a romantic Mills & Boon than sitting listening to your husband banging on about how there's nothing decent to eat in the airport for less than four quid.

Window or Aisle?

This is a tricky one. If you've got kids obviously it's better to have an aisle seat because they're gonna be up and down to the toilet weeing like an incontinent puppy. I don't know what it is but our Michael tries to drink non stop on a plane but I try and ration it out a bit, partly because you can't bring a flask from home anymore but are forced to pay bloody mental prices at the airport (THANKS Al Qaeda!), but also because he always wants the window seat so he can look out of it and let's face it, the last thing you want to start your holiday is a two and a half hour game of musical chairs.

Extra Leg Room

Unless you're a 7ft giant there really isn't any need for you to bother with this unwanted and frankly unnecessary expense. Plus, at £15 a pop with a family of four you'd have to be either rich or daft. Yes, these budget airline seats don't exactly put you in the lap of luxury but no pain, no gain as me mother said while giving birth to her seventh daughter (Olga, 10lbs 3oz). Also what's the point of moaning that after a two-hour flight you're not being able to move without assistance and can't feel your legs? My husband has that feeling every night in Benidorm.

Turbulance

I'm obviously not going to go into technical details of what turbulance is, mainly because I've no idea. Mel, my late father in law used to say it was something to do with "atmospheric pressure" (????!!!), Mick, my husband, says it's the airline buying cheap fuel that gets stuck in the exhaust. Whatever it is, the main rule here is DON'T PANIC. The first time our Mick flew we had terrible turbulence and he got bollocked by the airline staff for upsetting the other passengers. If fairness him running up and down the aisle screaming "we're going down, we're going down" then hammering on the pilot's door saying he wanted his money back was a bit offputting for the more experienced travellers. Sit tight with your seat belt securely fastened, hold on the those chair arms and grit your teeth. If the turbulence gets really bad and the plane starts going into freefall, the procedure is easy to remember: put your head between your knees and kiss your arse goodbye.

Lost Luggage

Once in a while an airline may lose your luggage. With this in mind, when travelling in winter make sure you wear clothing in lots of LAYERS so you can take off when you get to your resort. There's nowt worse than sitting on a sun bed waiting for your luggage to turn up looking like you're going to pass out in a heavy denim skirt and an Aran jumper. Also plain knickers and bra can sometimes pass for a bikini but be careful about going in the pool, the last thing you want is you getting out the shallow end and showing more muff than an Victorian lady trying to keep her hands warm.

Safe As Houses

Just a final note to say flying to your holiday destination is the safest form of travel known to man (or woman). I don't like to use the 'D' word but there is only one death in every 12.5 million flights worldwide every year. So you're actually more likely to win the big one on the National Lottery (odds: 14 million to 1) than you are snuffing it on an Easyjet flight from Manchester to Alicante. So keep flying and keep enjoying your holidays in the sun! (Oh, and if you DO win the lotto jackpot I'd start travelling by boat if I were you...)

SPOT THE DIFFERENCE

DIFFERENCE 3

Did you spot the difference?

Answer on page 152

WANTED
DEAD OR ALIVE
ENRIQUE 'THE RAT' LOPEZ

€10,000 REWARD

FOR FULL DETAILS OF REWARD CONTACT BENIDORM POLICE STATION

DO NOT BE FOOLED BY HIS LOW BROW AND MULLET HAIR, THIS IS NO VILLAGE IDIOT.
ENRIQUE 'THE RAT' LOPEZ IS A CRIMINAL MASTERMIND AND SHOULD NOT BE
APPROACHED, HE IS KNOWN TO BE ARMED AND DANGEROUS.

Health And Safety Incident Report

Incident Date: 22nd September 2007
Incident time: Aprox 3:30pm
Incident Location: Bullring
Incident Event: Solana Day Trip (Incorporating Juice Boost Blaster 2000 demo)
Person(s) involved: Mr Mel Harvey
Injury sustained: Electrocution

Summary of Incident:

The annual Solana free trip to the bull fight demonstration (incorporating Juice Boost Blaster 2000 demo) was going according to plan. I had successfully sold one Juice Boost Blaster (as per Solana Day Trip Guidelines) and had escorted the party to the bull ring where the bull fight demonstration was about to begin. Our regular bullfighter Senor Jose Carrasquillo was once again indisposed (please see H & S report dated 3rd August 2006 – "Alcoholic Bullfighter goes fucking mental") so Mr Mateo Castellanos once again agreed to step into his shoes (literally). Mr Castellanos was approximately 2/3 of the way through his bullfight demonstration with Peepo the dog when there was an extremely loud crash and electrical surge coming from the juicing room. On rushing back to the juicing room we found Mr Harvey lying prostitute on the floor covered in juice (mainly carrot, smatterings of pineapple). Mr Harvey was then pronounced dead by Mrs Kate Weedon (unqualified) whereupon I instructed Mr Castellanos to fetch an ambulance. As he did this and a sheet was placed over the deceased's body suddenly Mr Harvey sat bolt upright (causing at least one holiday maker to soil themselves) and asked, "What's happened? Have I missed the bullfight?" I would like to point out that in 20 years working for the Solana group I have never, ever had a resident shit themselves before (with one possible exception, please see H&S report dated 5th September 2006). Mr Harvey was offered to be dropped off at the Levante hospital on the way back to the Solana but categorically refused.

Signed:

Janey Mane.

Witnessed by:

Mateo

SOLANA

The mucho macho

It does not matter if you are on holiday, at work or at play, a macho look is very important. Especially if you are a man. Here are my best macho looks. If you are a guy feel free to copy my style and my attitude. And ladies, you know where to find me ...

looks of Mateo

Look #1
WAITER BAIT

This is mainly a work look, it says "I am hot and I can make coffee". The expression of the face tells the ladies I am not interested (see my article "Mateo's Guide to Holiday Romance"), the badge is not straight, this tells my employer I do not care and I am cool. Notice the hand, drawing your eye towards my *cojones*; gentlemen, believe me, it pays to advertise.

Look #2
STRONG LIKE BULL

This is my matador look. A matador is a fearless warrior always ready to do battle. You can see the determination on my face, this is a very hot look. I am making this look macho and cool even though I am wearing pink, a colour usually associated with homosexual gays.

This is my water aerobics look. I will be honest, at first I did not like this look, I thought it was not macho. Then I saw the reaction from the ladies and OMG (this is a cool way of saying "Jesus Christ!"), I have worn out my "Matkini" and now have two more in different styles. As you can see, this look is so hot I need a headband to keep me cool. Again, the hand draws attention to the "money".

This look is so hot the publishers said they could not use it. I said, "Don't be pussies, if we do not show my hottest looks how are the flabby, pale, ugly British guys reading this going to know to better themselves?" Of course they agreed. You know I am not a homosexual gay but sometimes I see this pic and think if there was two of me, I probably could be.

The mucho macho

Look #5
SPEC-TACULARLY HOT

Everyone knows it is looks girls go for and not brains. But if they cannot get a hot man they go for an ugly man who is clever. Imagine when they see a hot guy who is so clever he has to wear glasses?! You guessed it, you have one crazy chickita with a tidal wave in her bikini bottoms.

Look #6
PRETTY HOT

Wait, where did you get this picture? Are you crazy?? This is not one of the picture I gave you … This … this is a picture of er … my sister, yes, my sister. Her name is er … Fangita, she is hot but shouldn't be here. Please remove this picture before printing. I have another picture of me dressed as a motorcyle cop singing "Y.M.C.A." Very hot …

looks of Mateo

COMING SOON TO BENIDORM...

Kenneth's

MOBILE HAIR & BEAUTY SALON

Award winning Liverpool stylist *Kenneth du Beke* brings his legendary flair and artistry to the Costa Blanca. Whether you want a quick blow and go or a full head of highlights Kenneth is your man. With over five years' experience under **'Troy of Derby'** (East Midlands premier hair and beauty salon) Kenneth has carefully honed his skills with a pair of scissors and offers you a bespoke experience with one aim: to give you truly fabulous hair.

Kenneth's personal hair and beauty treatments include:

★ HIGHLIGHTS ★ LOWLIGHTS ★ HAIR EXTENSIONS ★ MANICURE ★ PEDICURE
★ PERSONAL WAXING ★ COFFEE ENEMAS (FROM MELLOW BIRDS TO COLOMBIAN FRESH GROUND)

NEW IN 2011, FOR THE DISCERNING HOMOSEXUAL, SOUP & HOOP

Kenneth will discreetly pop round on his Vespa 125 Sport, put the kettle on and make you a cup-a-soup of your choice while he goes to work waxing your back entrance until it's clean as a whistle! Satisfaction guaranteed!

Call Kenneth today on +34 0887 89887

Kenneth is currently looking for permanent premises in the Benidorm area. If you can help please email on Kennethdubeke@hotmail.co.uk

"ON A CHEWSDEE"

Janey

Full name:
Janey Yorke.

Place & date of birth:
Liverpooooul although you'd never guess from me acqhcent. On a Chewsdee.

Occupation:
Bar and entertainments manageress of a laaaarge, Spanish holadee resort.

Favourite holiday destination & why?
You've got to be fookin' joekun', when do I have time for da? Last 'olliedee I had Noah was the friggin' cruise rep.

Favourite food?
Anythin' as long as it's not da shite we give 'um here at the Solana.

Favourite type of music?
I don't mind a bit of tha what's his name, the blacgghk fella who died, Nat King Kong.

Which TV shows do you watch?
I quite like dem cooookery prowgrammes. I like dat fella who used to say "frig the chickunn in a basket, let's get pissed". Keith sumbodee. Keith Harris? No, he was the one with the parrot wasn't he? And you can piss off with that *Loose Women*, if I wanna sit n' listen to a load of moanin', middle aged slappers going threw the menopause I'll go up the bingo in the Hawaiian Function Room.

Do you have a role model?
Judi Dench. Face like a fookin bag of spanners but loved by everyone.

If you had to rate yourself 1–10 in attractiveness, how would you score?
Before the face lift about 6. After the facelift … About 6. Whadda waste of 800 Egyptian pounds dat was.

What has been your greatest accomplishment in life?
Gettin through each werkin day without fookin' slappin', punchin or stabbin' someone.

MICK GARVEY'S

Karaoke

MASTERCLASS

Who doesn't enjoy a night of karaoke? Nobody. Unless you count the people who are miserable, sober or music lovers. The word karaoke is actually Japanese for "couldn't give a shit" and that is exactly the attitude you need for this popular holiday pastime; to a point. Nobody wants to spend their evening in a foreign A&E unit nursing a burst eardrum after trying to hit the high note at the end of "Thunderball". Basically don't start to run before you can walk and where better to start than with my handy karaoke hints and tips.

BEGINNER

These songs are for beginners. You'll notice this category isn't titled "easy", there is no such thing as an easy karaoke song. Getting up in front of people with a microphone takes some bottle (about four does the trick for me, preferably San Miguel) and all of these songs require minimal singing ability but maximum personality. Look at Michael Crawford, his singing is shite but he gets away with it because he used to be in *Some Mothers Do Have 'Em*.

Two Little Boys – *Rolf Harris (Absolute classic, get this right & there won't be a dry eye in the house)*

D.I.V.O.R.C.E. – *Tammy Wynette (One for the bitter, gin soaked ladies)*

Ernie (The Fastest Milkman in The West) – *Benny Hill (Classic Novelty Song, watch your tempo, the lyrics "She lived all alone in Liddley Lane at number 22" have to be hit rhythmically and with purpose).*

CLASSICS

Who cares if you hit the right notes when the whole room is singing with you? Good confidence builders these.

Daydream Believer – *The Monkees (At just over 2½ mins this is also good if you get up on stage for the first time and kak yourself)*

American Pie – *Don McLean (Be warned, this song refuses to end)*

Sweet Caroline – *Neil Diamond (You can always rely on Neil for an easy sing but watch out for the key changes)*

I Will Survive – *Gloria Gaynor (Again, one for the ladies, probably avoid this if you are a bloke, unless of course you are a gay. Or don't mind people thinking you are a gay)*

My Way – *Frank Sinatra (A good one to end the night when everyone is hammered but be warned, if you wanna do this one get your slip in early, there's usually some old fart who comes in every night and does this and gets annoyed if somebody "pinches his song". A tip: when you hand in your slip if you are told "Oh, that's Harry's song" just say, "Yeah, he just said he doesn't wanna do it tonight and can you put him down for anything by Mika")*

EXPERT

I Will Always Love You – *Whitney Houston (The karaoke equivalent of a triple axel, the inexperienced will end up on their arses, covered in bruises)*

A Boy Named Sue – *Johnny Cash (Surprised to see this in the expert category? Yes, there's not a lot of singing in this Country classic but the lyrics go like shit off a stick, after a few bottles of beer you don't stand a chance)*

SONGS TO AVOID

Opera
Anything by Mika

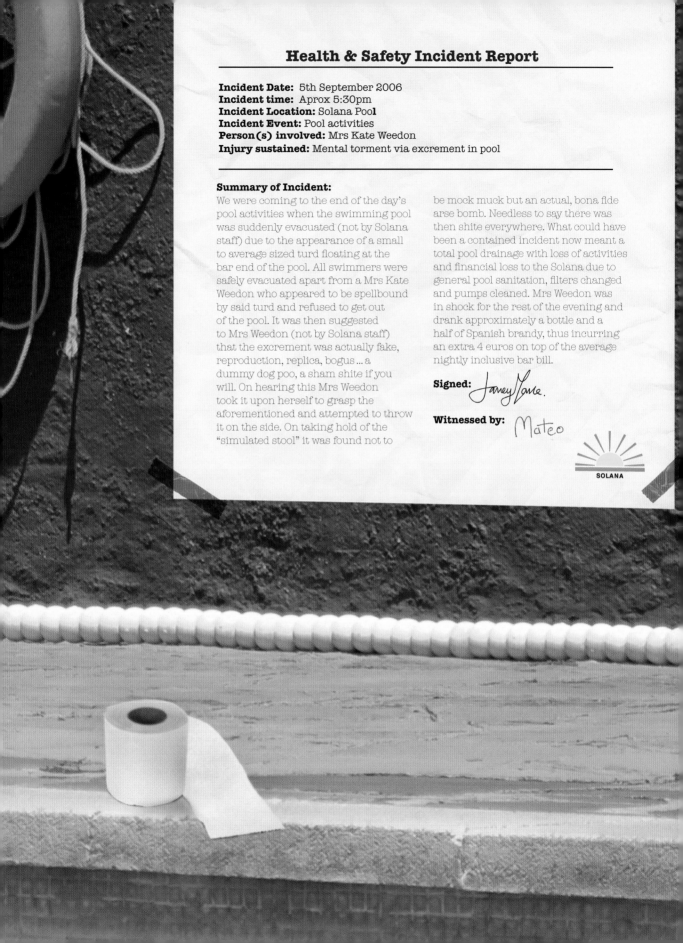

Health & Safety Incident Report

Incident Date: 5th September 2006
Incident time: Aprox 5:30pm
Incident Location: Solana Pool
Incident Event: Pool activities
Person(s) involved: Mrs Kate Weedon
Injury sustained: Mental torment via excrement in pool

Summary of Incident:

We were coming to the end of the day's pool activities when the swimming pool was suddenly evacuated (not by Solana staff) due to the appearance of a small to average sized turd floating at the bar end of the pool. All swimmers were safely evacuated apart from a Mrs Kate Weedon who appeared to be spellbound by said turd and refused to get out of the pool. It was then suggested to Mrs Weedon (not by Solana staff) that the excrement was actually fake, reproduction, replica, bogus ... a dummy dog poo, a sham shite if you will. On hearing this Mrs Weedon took it upon herself to grasp the aforementioned and attempted to throw it on the side. On taking hold of the "simulated stool" it was found not to be mock muck but an actual, bona fide arse bomb. Needless to say there was then shite everywhere. What could have been a contained incident now meant a total pool drainage with loss of activities and financial loss to the Solana due to general pool sanitation, filters changed and pumps cleaned. Mrs Weedon was in shock for the rest of the evening and drank approximately a bottle and a half of Spanish brandy, thus incurring an extra 4 euros on top of the average nightly inclusive bar bill.

Signed: *Janey Marie.*

Witnessed by: *Mateo*

SOLANA

"I'M IN MY LATE THIRTIES. VERY LATE THIRTIES"

Gavin

Full name:
Gavin Ramsbottom.

Place & date of birth:
I was born in Derby although you'd never know: Mother sent me to elocution lessons from an early age. I'm in my late thirties. Very late thirties.

Occupation:
Hair stylist.

Favourite holiday destination & why?
Where do I start? The waterways of Venice, the café society of Paris, the Ruins of Pollio Felice's Villa in Sorrento ... I've never been to any of them but one can dream. For the last few years I've been holidaying in Spain. Where we go is quite exclusive, it's a small fishing town on the Costa Brava, only 45 minutes from Alicante. I'd tell you the name of it but I fear it would only get overpopulated and eventually ruined.

Favourite food?
I try to watch what I eat as much as possible. I'm a serial dieter. At the moment I'm on the Chew-kan. You have to chew every mouthful at least fifty times. It's quite effective although eating soup can be a rather messy affair.

Favourite type of music?
I must admit I'm rather fond of musicals. Anything sung by American stage sensation Cheyenne Jackson is always guaranteed to perk me up no end.

Which TV shows do you watch?
Travelogues mainly. Michael Palin is a god in my eyes. Although I never really understood Monty Python but I suppose we all got a bit giddy in our youth.

Solana Memo

To: Janey
CC:
From: Mateo
Date & Time: Saturday 4pm

Haha, this is so funny that we can have this kind of joke at work, I like this. Haha ...

Janey I lobe you,

Mateo X

My Benidorm by Michael Garvey aged 11 ¾

Benidorm is brilliant, I go there with me family and it's great becuz we never have to pay for anything, except when me Dad breaks stuff and things like that but everythin else is free. They have a brilliant pool, sumbody said it's the best one in Benidorm and I can believe it cuz it's the best one I've ever been in. I've never been anywhere else that's got a swimming pool so I havent got much to compair it to but itz still good. Oh, I once did a shit in the pool but that was ages ago when I was a kid. It probably wasn't the best pool in Benidorm that day (but probably still wasn't the worst).

Not EVERYTHIN in Benidorm iz free, I just ment in the hotel where we stay, it's called The Solana which is Spanish for 'The Sun', me Dad said they named it after the newspaper because it's boring and full of tits but I think he was jokin, my Dadz always jokin. I'm pretty sure itz just named after the other sun, the one in the sky.

We've been to loads of places in Benidorm including a bullring, The Benidorm Palace (a sort of theatre where there's a show and you can have your dinner... me Grandad and Nana bought this place but then they lost it again, it's a long story) then a place where there are waterfalls (really cool), Peacock Island (an island in the middle of the sea that you can see from Benidorm), Terra Mittica (I think thatz how u spell it, it waz a theem park like alton towerz but betta) and my favourite place, the beach! I luved going to the beach but me Dad sez we can't go agen cuz it costs 2 much money. Plus some woman swizzed him out of a load of dosh to use the sun beds wen we wer ther + he went mental, he was already annoyed cuz he had to bye everyone ice creams.

Me Nana + Mel (me grandad) got marrid on Benidorm beech, it was brilliant. A fat bloke on a parrashoot came down and kicked me Grandad in the hed. We thort he mite hav killed him but he didnt, me grandad was ACE!

Anywayz, I dunno wot else to say about Benidorm so here are some cool picz from me holidayz LOL! I hope u like um!
Michael x

Here I am in the pool at the Solana, I think this looks weerd cuz Im a lot older now. And I dont look like a rabbit in a baseball cap any more LOL.

This is a pic me Dad took wile we woz on the beach. I think he only took it so he cud show uz eating the ice creams wot he payed for. Me Nana didnt like the beach at first cuz her mobility scooter wudnt work on the sand then me Mam sat her near a bin and she liked that.

This is a pic of me an me Nana an me an me mam. I waz a page boy or summut, I cant remember, once I chatted up a girl who was called Page but she stood me up. Benidorm isnt very good for meetin lassis.

This iz me grandad outside hiz shop he had in Benidorm. Mel (my grandad) waz brilliant, he died onXmaz day and I really miss him a lot.

This pic iz me at Terra Mittica, me Nana took this pic, Im dressed az a roman solger cuz they gave uz the costumez. All me matez at skool said I look well cool in thiz even tho a bit of it looks like a dress. But it aint a dress, itz a cool solger outfit. OK?!

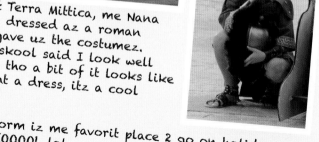

So basiclee, Benidorm iz me favorit place 2 go on holidey, u shud go 2 IT IZ KOOOOL lol.

KARAOKE

PRISON

Have an impending court case?
Looking like you will receive a
custodial sentence? Have a party!
You may as well while you can!

1. JAILHOUSE ROCK – *Elvis Presley*
2. WORKING ON A CHAIN GANG – *Sam Cooke*
3. GOING NOWHERE – *Oasis*
4. FOLSOME PRISON BLUES – *Johnny Cash*
5. ONLY THE LONELY – *Roy Orbison*
6. SMOOTH CRIMINAL – *Michael Jackson*
7. GETTING AWAY WITH MURDER – *Randy Crawford*
8. ARE YOU LONESOME TONIGHT? – *Elvis Presley*
9. OPEN WIDE THESE PRISON DOORS – *Neil Diamond*
10. I FOUGHT THE LAW – *The Clash*

Martin Weedon
66 The Villas
Shirley
Croydon

The Manager
Solana Resorts Int
Alicante
Spain

Dear Sir/Madam

In my life I have only once before been moved to write a letter of complaint, this was to the BBC protesting that my 130 letters to "Jim'll Fix It" had been constantly ignored over a three year period. I felt that my request for Jim to fix it for me to meet Pam Ayres was both cost effective and achievable yet despite these facts I was constantly overlooked and I did not receive one reply. I was eight years old (eleven when my campaign ended). I only mention this because this is my fifth letter of complaint to you and I still have yet to receive any form of discourse.

I have had the dubious "pleasure" of staying at the Benidorm Solana on three occasions now. The first time my wife and I were forced to book a budget holiday and your hotel fell into our price range, the second time we booked into a much nicer hotel but were moved to The Solana whereupon the hotel was taken hostage by international criminals. The third time I was given a voucher for a free holiday after the hostage incident the year before.

During these three stays with your company I have been subjected to an exploding juice extractor, (resulting in near death for another holiday maker), excrement in swimming pools and theft of my passport and all possessions. Your staff have been consistently rude, unhelpful, vulgar, dismissive, inefficient, disorganised and on at least one occasion slept with my wife and my mother (not at the same time). I hold your company totally responsible for the breakdown of my marriage and subsequent monthly psychiatry bill of approximately £240.

Let me be absolutely clear, I don't expect any admission of responsibility, all I want is a reply. Some form of acknowledgement that lets me know I'm not just screaming into the wind. Perhaps you could just send a scrap of paper with the words "we got your letter" or "OK" or even "screw you", it wouldn't be the first time you've done that to me (and my wife and mother).

I'm begging of you, reply to this letter. I need some form of closure before I go completely and irreversibly insane.

Yours sincerely

M. Weedon.

M Weedon

SOLANA, BENIDORM
SOLANA RESORTS INTERNATIONAL
HOTEL BILL

6TH OCTOBER 2011

Thank you for choosing Solana. We hope you enjoyed your holiday, considering the amount of noise you made we can only assume you did. Here is your final invoice.

	€18
Breaking of plastic chair x 2	€5
Destruction of ping pong bat	€60
Vandalism to karaoke microphone	€22
Irreparable devastation to bed linen	
Soiling of Swimming pool	€400
(includes new sanitiser, filtration system and chemicals)	
	€505
TOTAL	

**PLEASE DO NOT ATTEMPT TO LEAVE BEFORE SETTLING YOUR BILL,
WE HAVE YOUR PASSPORTS.**

Janey Yorke
Solana Manageress

SPOT
THE
DIFFERENCE

In this picture Janice is
thinking about what she's
going to wear that evening,

in this picture, she is not.

Apart from the obvious changes in the
picture composition,

in this picture Mateo has
unfortunately shat himself.

There is absolutely no difference
whatsoever.

Each picture is totally devoid
of dignity.

Donald & Jacqueline's guide to a happy marriage

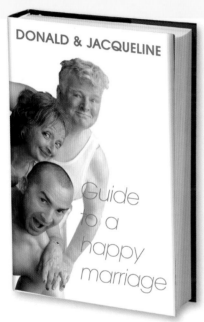

First of all we would like to thank the lovely Stan Collymore for writing the foreword to our first little hardback. We first met Stanley in a car park in Ashby de la Zouch; he's such a character; we'd heard on the swinging circuit that he can be a bit of a handful and I must admit after that warm summer's evening in his Ford Transit, Jacqueline can certainly vouch for that! But seriously, we've met a lot of people over the years (A LOT of people!) but Mr C has proved to be a real one off, a gentleman and a scholar who has certainly added a splash of colour into our lives (huge cock as well!).

OK, that's the housekeeping out of the way, on with show…

Hola!!!!!

Well, we must admit we were a bit taken aback when we were approached by Constable & Robinson to write a marriage guidance book. At first we thought the letter was from Elaine Constable and Eric Robinson, two lovely friends from the Gorbals; Elaine was one of Scotland's most successful lap dancers but is now unfortunately wheelchair bound following an accident while performing covered in baby oil on scaffolding at the re-opening of Erskine Bridge in 1996.

HARD TO SAY NO!

Eric, on the other hand is one of the UK's most successful Erotic Jugglers ("Eric Robinson – A Juggler With Balls!") and still plays a huge role in Scotland's vibrant swinging scene. Anyway, turns out Constable & Robinson are publishers and we were being asked to impart the secrets of our long and happy marriage in book form and as you can see, we found it hard to say no! (Jacqueline rarely does).

COCK-OH-VAN TO TOED IN YOUR HOLE

Within these pages you will find the secret to a long and happy union. They say variety is the spice of life and we can guarantee more spice than a beef vindaloo (by the way, never serve beef vindaloo at a swingers' meeting. Spillages can be quite eye watering and come the early hours you'll need more windows open than an advent calendar on Christmas Eve, if you know what I mean – it's a mistake we'll only make the once!).

friend Big-Jugs Jenny often says after a good strap-on session). We favour a delightful Spanish village called Benidorm which you will find along the costal road from Alicante. We strongly feel 'all inclusive' is the way forward, as far as holidays go, and never take any cash with us. Self service also means you don't have to hand out any of those hellishly expensive "gratuities" to waiters etc (although Jacqueline has been known to get the odd "big tip" on the beach after dark!).

JACQUELINE LOVES THE "GAYS" AND I MUST SAY I HAVE A SOFT SPOT FOR THEM TOO

Talking of Benidorm there is a small but extremely informative article about "being a gay" in this book written by our good holiday chums Gavin and Troy (this section appropriately found towards the rear). Jacqueline loves the "gays" and I must say I have a soft spot for them too; after all, there is no better way your partner can show their love for you than by letting you "park your car around the back" (if you know what I mean).

So welcome to "Donald & Jacqueline's Guide to A Happy Marriage". With our help you can make yours a very long and enjoyable one (and we can give advice on your marriage too!).

Love

Donald
Jacqueline
xx

In saying that, near the middle of the book you will find some wonderful recipes which are suitable for a fruity evening in with broadminded friends; from Cock-oh!-Van (thanks to Stan C for that one) to Toed-in-your-hole – not forgetting details on how to host a Finger Buffet (no food required for that one).

BIG-JUGS JENNY AFTER A GOOD STRAP-ON SESSION

Obviously we have a holiday section too; Jacqueline and I are creatures of habit and will be imparting ways to enjoy the same holiday at the same time, year in year out. If it ain't broke don't fix it (as our

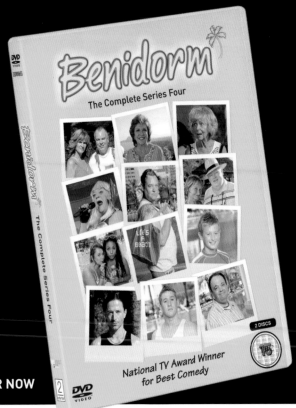